TRUE WHIT

TRUE WHIT

DESIGNING A LIFE OF STYLE, BEAUTY, AND FUN

Whitney Port

with Sheryl Berk

First published in Great Britain
2011 by Aurum Press Ltd
7 Greenland Street
London NW1 0ND
www.aurumpress.co.uk

Published by arrangement with HarperCollins Publishers,
10 East 53rd Street, New York, NY 10022.

A catalogue record for this book is available from the British Library.

ISBN 978 1 84513 673 4

1 3 5 7 9 10 8 6 4 2
2011 2013 2015 2014 2012

Designed by Ashley Halsey
Printed in the Untied States of America

To the family whose love has given me the will and the courage to fly.
To Mommy, Daddy, Bucka, Boppa, Ry, Ash, Paige, and Jade:
Your love has brought harmony to my life.
Without you this dream would not be alive.

CONTENTS

TRUE WHIT

INTRODUCTION

My mom always called it the "quarter-life crisis," the time in your life when you're in your twenties, out of school, and facing the world on your own for the first time. To be honest, it didn't sound like a crisis to me; it sounded pretty great. Freedom, an amazing career, finding the man of my dreams . . . I couldn't wait to be on my own. I could do what I wanted, be what I wanted, dress like I wanted, and spend my money on *anything*. Crisis? It sounded like heaven!

So in August 2008, a year after finishing college at the University of Southern California, I packed up my clothes, shoes, and accessories (enough to probably fill two apartments!) and moved to New York City to start my life and make it as a fashion designer. I found my first place in the Flatiron District, and the freedom felt incredible. Okay, it wasn't exactly the sophisticated New York apartment I'd envisioned. In fact, it was on the thirtieth floor (I am semiscared of heights), the ceilings were superlow, and my closet was the size of a shoebox. But it was still mine, all mine, and my first night in it, I felt invincible. I furnished it by scouring the floors of ABC Carpet, hitting up the local flea market and thrift shops, shopping online for basic must-haves, as well as finding some of the accessories at antique stores in Osage Beach, Missouri (a spot my family has traveled to since the year I was born).

I distinctly remember lighting a candle, ordering Chinese food, and using boxes as tables to have a romantic night with my boyfriend when I first moved in.

I was lucky in these tough financial times to also land a job right away as a public relations assistant for the Diane von Furstenberg brand. DVF is such an incredible designer, I simply wanted to work there and was willing to do anything and everything just to be a part of the team. However, my job was not exactly the glamorous fashion position I'd imagined. It consisted of a lot of assistant tasks—like searching the media for celebs wearing DVF, dressing the mannequins, assisting in seating charts for runway shows—and required little creativity. I felt like I was going nowhere fast. At twenty-three years old, I shouldn't have expected much more responsibility; I just knew I was capable of so much more. Don't get me wrong: I owe DVF immensely for her words of empowerment and the time she spent making sure I followed my dreams. But . . .

After a few weeks of experiencing my newfound freedom, I began to think maybe Mama was on to something. Being on my own wasn't as easy as I thought. The real world is filled with challenges, expectations, pressure, and to be honest, more than a few crazy people. I wish they taught a class on this in college: Real Life 101. Maybe then I would have known what to expect and how to handle it with grace and style and less stress. Instead, I had to find my way. I had to experience firsthand what it's like to be in a relationship with Mr. Not Quite Right and to work with someone vying for the title "Wicked Witch of the East." I had to stuff envelopes and answer phones and fetch coffee and steam fabric and lug bins of clothes. And even harder: I had to figure out how to look *good* even when things were really bad.

There were times I would have loved to just throw in the towel, to crawl back home to my parents and be a kid again with no responsibilities, no rent to pay, no repercussions for showing up five minutes late to a work meeting without a pen. I wish someone would have warned me that bills pile up, jobs are never as good as they sound on Monster.com, and not everyone at the office is nice (some are shockingly biased and backstabbing!). Sometimes I didn't know who to trust or where to turn. I missed the comforts of college and home; I felt anxious, overwhelmed, *alone.* One day, I woke up in a cold sweat wondering, *where am I going? And will I ever get there?* I was in . . . a crisis.

But here's the kicker: I got to experience my quarterlife crisis in front of *millions* of people every week! MTV's *The City* is a great show, and I'm really proud of it, but it's also *really* revealing. Sometimes, I feel like I'm living in a fishbowl and there are things, frankly, I wish the whole wide world didn't have to see. Most of the week, I have cameras in my face filming everything—and I mean *everything*. The good, the bad, and the "Oh, my God! I can't believe I did that!" So there I was, new to New York, being on my own and working while the cameras captured me failing, falling on my butt, and freaking out. The producers were probably thrilled—I became a drama magnet and I always said I never would be one. I even lived out a serious relationship and painful breakup over several episodes. As my friend Roxy Olin would say, "Only you, Whit, only you . . ."

Think of this book as your road map to discovering what you want in life and how to make it happen.

But it's not *only* me. I know that it's my real-life problems that so many girls relate to—they tell me so all the time. They say they're rooting for me, and because of that, I can't give up. So that's what I did: I took a deep breath and reassessed. I made good friends and weeded out the frenemies. I tried three new jobs until I found one that felt right. I decided to pursue my original dream of being in fashion, even if it meant taking a huge leap of faith and risking failure. I surrounded myself with a support team who believed in me, and even better, I discovered how important it was to believe in myself. If you stay true to who you are, you'll eventually (I promise!) stumble across the right path.

So that's the road I am hopefully on now. If you've watched me on *The Hills* or *The City*, you know it hasn't been easy getting here, and I absolutely expect more bumps along the way. But what you've seen on the shows is only the half of it; many of my experiences wind up on the cutting-room floor (we only have thirty minutes per episode, after all). So this book is the *true* Whit: all the situations I've been through and survived, all the solutions that worked for me as well as the ones that didn't. I felt there was so much more that I could share beyond what you see on the show. What I wanted to create was a guidebook, so to speak, to starting out in your twenties. This is a hard time in your life to navigate—sometimes it can feel impossible to have fun and not stress out while you're trying to get the hang of being "a grown-up." It was particularly hard for me, because I live most of my life in the public view. If I stayed out all night with friends partying, not only would I have my boss and coworkers to contend with in the morning, I also knew the cameras would be rolling. This forced me to learn some tricks for quick makeup and hair (I can put my face on in five minutes flat, I swear!). Then there's the *really* useful stuff you need to know, like how to recover from a hangover, find the perfect outfit when you're having dinner with an ex, and throw a fabulous last-minute dinner party using just a toaster oven!

Starting out is like being on a roller coaster. You know there are going to be some terrifying twists and turns, and you might feel scared or even sick to your stomach at times, but the thrill of the ride takes your breath away.

If you're anything like me, you've probably got a million questions: "What's my passion? "Where do I want to be in five years?" "*Now* what?" I can't answer these questions for you, but I can give you some great tools to start figuring them out. I've also been lucky enough throughout my journey so far to have met really dynamic people who are really good at what they do: stylists, trainers, business execs—and also my friends and family. They're all in here, sharing their words of wisdom. They are the roots that have allowed me to grow.

People are always asking me for advice (I guess that's what I get for being on a reality TV show!): "Whitney, what should I do now that I've graduated from college?" Well, here (after much personal trial and error!) is what I have to say to that:

- Dream big, dearies, and dress the part!
- Live the life you love and don't be afraid to take chances!
- Be fabulous, be fearless, be yourself!

And yes, you're going to screw up. I sure did, and I will continue to do so. But that's okay. Mistakes are good things, even if they don't feel like it at the time (try to remember that when you're sobbing on the phone to your bestie). They make you wiser and stronger. They help put things into perspective, like what really counts (the people you love who love you back) and what really doesn't (your burned dinner, your fashion faux pas, your flaky blind date). They teach you how to cope and not crumble.

You also need to give yourself a break. *Seriously!* There seems to be this big misconception that because you're in your twenties and a "grown-up" now, you're supposed to have your entire life figured out. That's *so* not true; I know very few twentysomethings who have all their stuff together. Up until now—for the past twenty-plus years—your entire life has been on a strict schedule. So this is the first time you're calling the shots. Of course you're confused; of course you're freaking out. But you should also be excited to get started! It's your time to shine, to dig deep and discover who you are. This is the first time you're going to be making important choices not based on what your peers, your parents, or anyone else thinks or expects of you. *You* are in control.

Once I realized this, I felt completely empowered, and I was ready to face my future. I figured out a game plan, and I try to stick to it. Think about it like this: starting out is like being on a roller coaster. You know there are going to be some terrifying twists and turns, and you might feel scared or even sick to your stomach at times, but the thrill of the ride takes your breath away.

Buckle your seat belts . . . let's get started!

XOXO

whit

CHAPTER ONE

HOME SWEET HOME

For me, moving out was a huge step. It wasn't just about getting my own space and decorating it. My home was going to be a place I could call my own and be myself, a space where I could decompress after a hectic day and shed the layers. Emotionally, it meant I was breaking away from my parents, following my calling, and establishing what my life was really going to be about. I did a lot of talking about how I was an adult, but I didn't fully feel like one until I was out from under my parents' roof. College was the first time I had my own apartment, but it was still part of a safe community, with rules and boundaries and support.

My first apartment left a lot to be desired. It was dark and had the closet space of a Barbie town house; if I wore my four-inch stilettos and put my hair up, my head practically brushed the ceiling. It was far from a glamorous abode, but with a little ingenuity (and a whole lot of creativity), I transformed it into a space I was proud to call home—and wouldn't be mortified to have friends and family visit.

I tackled my decorating much in the same way I would approach putting together a great fashion ensemble: I mixed a little bit of this with a little bit of that, paired comfy classics with vintage or thrift-shop steals, and spiced it up with some color and bold accents. I am even known to use my own accessories like headbands and necklaces as interior design pieces. And, of course, I made sure to "Whitneyfy" it! I love to mix and match patterns; it's my funky twist on being eclectic. I really love an Art Deco kind of look that blends vintage and modern. *Architectural Digest* might never consider my apartment cover material, but that's okay. I loved how I made it my own on my budget.

IT'S ALL ABOUT YOU

Here's your opportunity to finally make your living space all your own. Own your identity! For your whole life, you've lived in a home filled with someone else's vision. You can finally let that inner interior designer out and make it as simplistic or ornate as you wish. Every square inch should reflect your personality, your taste, your essence. Yes, you want guests to ooh and aah when they come over. But frankly, you have to live here. Every day, every night. You have to feel comfortable; you have to feel inspired, relaxed, rejuvenated. Sure, white carpeting might look cool—but *hello*? Who's gonna clean it every time you track in some dirt on your shoes? I purposely chose a dark brown carpeting for this reason—one of my pet peeves is dirty carpet.

This is my first New York City apartment in the Flatiron District. I loved the floor-to-ceiling windows and the views—although it certainly looked bare before I decorated!

Take a good look around you—try to see the possibilities, not the problems. Don't just dwell on what your new dwelling is lacking (windows, closets, a corner of wall that is not peeling . . .). Instead, focus on the positives (It's cute and cozy!

The fridge and oven work! There's a pizza joint that delivers 24/7 down the block!). Like I said, my first place was no palace. I knew there was a ton to be done. But the idea of transforming something is exciting. You're doing your own *Extreme Home Makeover!*

You have to feel comfortable; you have to feel inspired, relaxed, rejuvenated.

At first, I bought things based on aesthetics. But then I quickly realized that although that's fun, and it's very easy to get carried away if something catches your eye, function and form really count. You should be able to collapse on your couch and put your feet up at the end of the day without worrying about ruining anything. So by all means, buy pieces that "speak" to you—but just make sure they're usable as well.

I did a lot of thinking before I started decorating. I made a list (I make lots of lists—they're my secret weapon!). I knew what I needed: some creative ways to brighten things up and create the illusion of light and airiness. I wanted color. I am a California girl at heart, even if I am living in the heart of NYC. Dreary, dark, and

drab are not in my vocab. My apartment in New York could technically be considered a rainbow: my dining room table sits on top of a multicolor-striped carpet; I have a blue, purple, and green floral chair in my living room, and vases of every color. Plus, my bedroom is painted lavender . . . and my bed is black and white!

Think about everything you want your home to embody. What are the words you want to use to describe your dream dwelling? Cozy and comfy? Chic and sleek? Functional? Funky? Keep those words in mind as you shop. And remember, patience is a virtue. Rome wasn't built in a day; likewise, your first apartment. It takes some time (maybe even an eternity) to fully decorate your space. And just when you think you're totally done . . . you change your mind and redo everything to create a new vibe, or you move out! Go ahead—have fun furnishing. That's the best part of having your own home: no one is going to tell you that chintz and plaid clash or that old 45s are not artwork.

And if you don't have a lot of money to decorate, no problem. Most of my favorite furnishings cost me next to nothing. You know that feeling when you find a stunning pair of shoes on the sale rack in your size? That's how I felt filling my home with inexpensive, unique, and exciting accents I got for a steal. *Score!*

DECORATING ON A BUDGET

No funds to furnish? Never fear, dear . . .

- **Somebody's trash can be** someone else's treasure. In every town there are countless thrift shops, flea markets, or yard/garage sales. Vintage pieces are some of the best finds I have. I nabbed my white leather dining room chairs at the thrift shop right next to my building in New York, as well as a colorful, floral-patterned comfy chair for my living room. I also go to Missouri every summer and browse the antique shops with my mom—that's where I pick up most of my lamps and vases. If I see something I like, I haggle! I will drive an hour outside town to this farmhouse that auctions everything off—from dish sets to bicycles, board games to John Deeres! It's a blast, and some of my favorite pieces come from these trips.

At seven years old with my two grandmothers: on the right is Grandma Nana, Dad's mama, and on the left is Grandma Bucka, Mom's mom.

It may sound gross, but this chair was actually left in my apartment by my predecessors.

- **Swapping furniture and home accessories** with friends is a great way to get rid of your clutter while also bringing new life into your space. Compile what you are willing to give up, then get together and do some fair trading!

- **Search a family member's garage or basement.** My grandmother is a huge collector of antiques, and over the years I have taken/been given vases, tea sets, lamps, candy dishes. My apartment has benefited from Gram's great finds!

- **Bright and bold colors** add drama where you want it; cool pastels soothe and calm. Slapping on a fresh coat of paint is a quick and easy fix. And I don't just mean the walls; don't be afraid to take a spray can to a dull piece of furniture to spruce it up.

- **Wallpaper is another great option;** anthropologie.com has some cool, unusual patterns—paper that looks like lace, letters, even silverware! Or, if you're artistically inclined, turn your walls into your own personal canvas. In my old college apartment, I would just take a marker to the wall and start doodling a design. If you—or anyone you know—has artistic ability, this is a great way to add bursts of color and whimsy to plain walls. Another trick I love: putting up bright swatches of fabric using pushpins. They won't damage the walls if you're worried about your landlord, and you can change the fabric to suit any mood or occasion.

I found this beautiful antique bar set in Osage Beach, too!

- **Can't afford new furniture?** Some inexpensive accessories can transform old pieces. Brighten up your old couch with funky pillows or a snazzy throw, and your ratty sofa is suddenly transformed! Need extra seats for entertaining? My best friend from childhood, Joanna Scapa, creatively scattered multicolored cushions around her living room floor. Practical *and* cool!

- **Camouflage floor or carpet** stains by throwing down some rug remnants. Mix colors, textures, even shapes. I even found a fab fake white fur rug at Costco!

- **Spruce up a boring bathroom** with a new shower curtain, some vibrant hand towels, and bath accessories. All can be found for cheap at places like Bed Bath and Beyond, Anthropologie, or Urban Outfitters, and they really make a difference. I'm also a huge fan of the Simply Shabby Chic for Target line. The white damask bathroom accessories feel pretty and feminine and cost under $20! You can even buy online!

- **Framed personal photos** make any space more special. I like to buy cheap frames and embellish them (you can hot-glue on gems, beach glass, shells, wine corks, buttons . . . just refrain from elbow macaroni, unless you're going for that elementary school look). You can also pull pages out of a vintage book or magazine and put them up in ready-made matted frames. Instant art collection! My favorite source for old books is the Strand in Union Square in NYC—but any used bookshop will have great options, or check out cheapbooks.com or half.com. Sometimes, you can pick up dozens of books for less than a dollar each! I just snatch up a batch with colorful covers or spines, not even looking at the titles, and scatter them on shelves and tabletops to add some interest to the room.

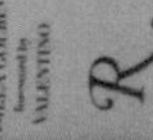

- **Simple window treatments** instantly make a room look more luxe. You can pick up some inexpensive curtains or swags of fabric and hang them wherever you need a bit of color. Or if you know how to sew, buy some pretty fabric and hem it to hang on a rod. Suddenly, those plain white walls of your living room come to life!

- **Chalkboard paint can turn a wall or a portion of a wall into a full-on chalkboard.** You can keep a constant visual to-do list, visitors can draw and leave you messages, or you can go crazy and draw as you please. Get different-color chalk and go nuts!

- **Hit up your local fabric store** to re-cover a piece of furniture that has great bones but maybe needs a new vibe. Restain, re-paint, and re-cover. Voilà! Instant masterpiece. Usually re-covering a piece of furniture is cheaper and easier than buying something completely new.

An antique find in Osage Beach, Missouri, where my family vacations.

YOUR CLOSET IS THE SIZE OF A SHOEBOX

I admit I am not the most organized person on the planet—probably because I spend a lot of time traveling and living out of suitcases (Excuses! Excuses!). But I do use every inch—and I mean every inch—of my space. I like to put space dividers in my drawers so I can separate out my undies, socks, tights, and bras. I also create categories in my closet: pants are hung together; likewise jackets, shirts, dresses, and skirts. And each category gets a different color hanger—so I can grab for red and know that the mini skirt I need is right there. And I do have one golden rule: put things away. That means no tossing stuff any which way into drawers (resulting in a future game of hide-and-seek), no piling clothes to the ceiling or leaving them on the floor. My mom always told me it takes just as little time to hang something up as it does to throw it on the floor. So true! And I'm much happier when my bedroom doesn't look like a tornado hit it.

I'm much happier when my bedroom doesn't look like a tornado hit it.

There are many affordable and easy ways to store your stuff. Places like the Container Store, Target, Walmart, Bed Bath and Beyond, and so on, have amazingly cheap products that will help you maximize and compartmentalize.

- **Risers for your bed are a great option** because they create a whole new storage space. You can store your winter clothes in summer and vice versa. Invest in some under-the-bed storage boxes or bags. The ones that vacuum-seal your sweaters flat are especially great for tight spaces.

- **Get the skinniest hangers you can;** the skinnier the hangers, the more of them you can have! If you're superpressed for space, use multitiered hangers to group skirts and pants together, or a rod that hangs from an existing one to create double the rack room.

- **Rotate seasonal clothes** front and center at eye level. For example, in the spring/summer, winter clothes should be placed out of ready-reach so your pretty sundresses are easy to find. Have sweaters and coats laundered or dry-cleaned (be sure to empty all pockets) and consider storing them so you have more room.

- **Clip-on shelf dividers** are a great way to keep sweaters, hats, purses, shoes, and gloves separated and accessible. Or try using inexpensive wicker baskets on shelves or on the floor of your closet for storing accessories. A small towel rack hung on the inside of your closet door is perfect for keeping scarves tidy; a hanger with multiple three-ring-binder-type metal rings will hold belts and keep them in line.

- **Be creative with how you store your jewelry.** I have a small bowl next to my bed and I drop all the little things—like stud earrings and rings that I wear all the time—into it. I also have a mannequin in my apartment that I use to drape fabric, and she often gets adorned with my accessories. It's like a big paper doll! In my dresser, I have tons of boxes and trays of necklaces, earrings, and rings. Some other great

ideas: use the necks of wine bottles to stack a collection of bangle bracelets; pick up an inexpensive tackle box and keep jewelry neat and tidy inside. I also love the idea of using an artist's wooden modeling hands to hold rings, bracelets, and so on. Whimsical and efficient!

- **Invest in instant "footwear files"** by buying a vertical shoe organizer; one that hangs over the back of the closet door will give you more room than one that sits on the closet floor—and it doesn't take up floor space. I categorize my shoes into boots, sandals, flats, close-toed heels, and open-toed heels and store them either on shelves or in an over-the-door rack. Sometimes, it simply helps to see what's inside the box. You can shoot Polaroids of your shoes and tape them to the boxes, or invest in see-through

plastic boxes so you can find your mules in minutes.

- **I have tons of hair accessories** that can disappear if they're not well organized. I have a wrought-iron headband tree next to my bed. Bundles of barrettes? No prob. Clip them to a long ribbon (you can hang it up inside your closet door) so they won't wander away. Or simply tuck them in snack-size plastic bags, according to color or clip style, and store in a drawer.

LET THERE BE LIGHT!

A lot of apartments don't come with overhead lighting or even good natural light. In fact, my first two apartments didn't have any overhead lights at all. Good thing for me I love dim light—I think it's romantic and relaxing. But when you need to see and want to brighten up a dark room:

- **Keep walls and floors light;** it will instantly make the room look brighter and bigger. I love soft muted shades. In my first apartment, I did the living room in a light Tiffany blue color. In the bedroom of that apartment, I painted the wall behind my bed a dainty ballerina pink. Now my bedroom is a delicate lavender; it's so soothing. Lavender is one of my mom's fave colors, so when I am far away, it reminds me of her and home.
- **Forget dark furniture.** Go for warm, vibrant patterns on sofas and chairs. My couch is a turquoise paisley pattern. And try light-colored wood or white-finish furniture to brighten up the space and make it look bigger.
- **Wall sconces, table lamps, and floor lamps** that direct light up at the ceiling can help get rid of a cavelike atmosphere. Simple, cheap lamps are always easy to find either at Walmart, Target, ZGallerie.com, or a thrift

shop; and you can customize them with spray paint and new shades. I have actually accessorized some of my lamp shades with brooches, pins, and earrings to add a funky element to a simple shade.

- **Mirrors give the illusion of light** because they reflect it. They open up a room, virtually "doubling" it in size. Place a mirror on a wall opposite a set of windows and suddenly you have tons of natural light. Standing mirrors are also a great fix; they give the optical illusion of a bigger room.

- **Candles, candles, candles . . .** beyond adding twinkling light to the darkest atmosphere, they smell heavenly.

- **Get rid of old fluorescent bulbs** and replace them with soft white incandescent bulbs that will make the lighting seem more natural. Or try full-spectrum bulbs, which cost a bit more than regular incandescent bulbs, but which mimic the sun's natural light.

This hand-painted candle is one of my favorites! It features gorgeous peonies (my favorite flower) in bright colors, and smells like them, too. I got it from gracioushome.com—an amazing place for home furnishings and accessories.

YOUR BEDROOM IS YOUR OASIS

The room you sleep in should be a sexy, spiritual haven. Bad day at work, be gone! Nothing can bother me when I'm snuggled in my bed. Your bedroom is a place for you to escape and cocoon. My one hard-and-fast rule: I never bring my laptop into bed. Your bedroom should never be associated with work (only play!). My bedroom is lavender, with a black-and-white-patterned headboard (which was an antique room divider that my mom found), cream-colored bedding with hints of black and silver, a soft, white faux fur rug, lots of eclectic picture frames, and a floor mirror that has mother-of-pearl edging. I do basically *everything* in my bedroom: watch TV, read magazines, eat popcorn in bed (bad habit), dance around to music, put on my makeup, and style my hair. Even if you're in a studio apartment—and your bed is literally part of your living room—little touches can help you unwind and de-stress:

- **Your bed is your best friend** at the end of a long day. Invest in your comfort by purchasing a feather bed (it sits on top of the mattress giving it extra softness) and a plush down (or down-alternative) comforter. I went to Bloomingdale's with my mom to try it all out. In my opinion, thick and cushiony is the way to go. There is just nothing like sinking into a soft cloud. *Ahhh . . .*

- **Itchy sheets are a no-no.** If you can't afford a high thread count, do what I do: buy sheets in super-soft jersey T-shirt material. I love Pure Beech sheets at Bed Bath and Beyond. They come in every color imaginable and are as soft as a twenty-year-old T-shirt.

- **Have a plethora of pillows.** I sleep with four: two are in the tee material, two are in ultrasoft

Step into my boudoir . . . My cozy bed has lots of pillows, and extra blankets for extra comfort.

fleece. They remind me of comfy, fuzzy socks. Heaven! Thus two of the pillows are cold when I get in bed and two are warm. I know, I'm weird!

- **Scent your room.** Candles and reed diffusers fill your entire space with fragrance and are inexpensive. They help to set the mood for relaxing on a Sunday morning or help energize me for a night out. You can even go online and make your own scent at reeddiffusers.org. I love the scent of peonies and gardenias. One of my fave candles is by Votivo in "Clean, Crisp White." It smells like fresh laundry! I also love the scent of vanilla, peony, and anything by Diptyque.

- **Fill your room with fresh flowers or plants.** Pick them from outside or find a cheap bunch at the market; they put a smile on my face whenever I smell or see them. Lily of the valley, lavender, roses, narcissus, and lilacs are particularly fragrant. Roxy was staying at my apartment this weekend while I was away, and as a thank-you, she put a vase of peach roses next to my bed with a note. When I got home, it was like walking into a room filled with sunshine!

- **I live in my blanket** when I am in the comfort of my bedroom. Try to find a fleece fabric; you will never want to take it off. I just wrap it around myself. The ultimate Snuggie! When I'm home in L.A., my family makes fun of me for stealing all the blankets and wearing them around the house.

- **Are you a light person . . . or a dark one?** I personally love sunlight and moonlight streaming through my windows. If that's the case for you, choose gauzy, sheer curtains. They'll be cooler in the summer, too, allowing the breeze to stream in. If you must have total darkness to slumber, then invest in blackout shades (and a great sleep mask).

- **Decorate your bedroom with photos**. My mom hung pictures with clothespins on a clothesline in my sister's dorm room so that she could display all of her pictures without taking up too much space. It made my sister feel happy and at home—even when she was at college. Likewise, every ledge and tabletop in my apartment holds frames with pictures of my friends, family, and special occasions. If you've got too many photos to display individually, you can pick up a plain corkboard, wrap it in ribbon or fabric, and create your own memory board. Or pick up a digital frame with a large memory stick; this can hold hundreds of images! Scrapbooks are also fun, personal coffee-table books. I have scrapbooks from my friend Christina from college and my best friend, Andrea, as books on my living-room coffee table.

- **Color your room cozy.** Paint colors that are too bold or dark can be a distraction in your bedroom. They also make the space feel a lot smaller than it is. If you want to feel relaxed and peaceful, be sure that the color on the walls is neutral or pastel such as tan, cream, light blue, light pink, and light yellow. Avoid harsh colors like red, black, and dark green. Your bedding can be bolder, but keep it in the same color family; clashing colors will not soothe the nerves. Personally, I like more neutral, muted tones for the bed, shades of white, cream, nude, and pastels. But you should do what works for you.

- **I am all about texture: soft, fluffy, or floaty fabrics** that feel nice to the touch. You can mix and match them; shag rugs with flannel bedding; satin pillows with cotton sheets; a crocheted throw or cashmere-blend blankets over a silky duvet.

- **Bedroom lighting should be soft, calm, romantic.** No bright, blaring overheads. Fluorescent lighting is my ultimate nightmare. I'd rather shower or get ready in the dark with light from one candle than function under fluorescent. Think dim and delicate for drowsing. I also love candlelight in my bedroom. There's something about the soft flicker of the flame that lulls me to sleep.

STOCKING UP: WHAT EVERY GIRL NEEDS IN HER . . .

Stocking up is more than just filling your shelves, cabinets, or drawers with "stuff." It empowers you by helping you feel prepared for whatever comes your way. I may not be emotionally prepared for every scenario, but at least I know I have the right supplies to handle the situation—be it a flashlight, extra batteries, or some cough medicine. There's also something very "grown up" about planning for the future, and not just "winging it." When I felt a cold coming on recently, and my mom called to ask if I had everything I needed, I was proud to say, "Yup, I've got it all under control." And I wasn't just saying that: prewinter, I filled my medicine cabinet with cold and flu essentials, so if I was alone and feeling crappy, I didn't have to crawl out to the drugstore to get medicine. I still felt stuffy headed and sniffly for a few days, but I reveled in my independence!

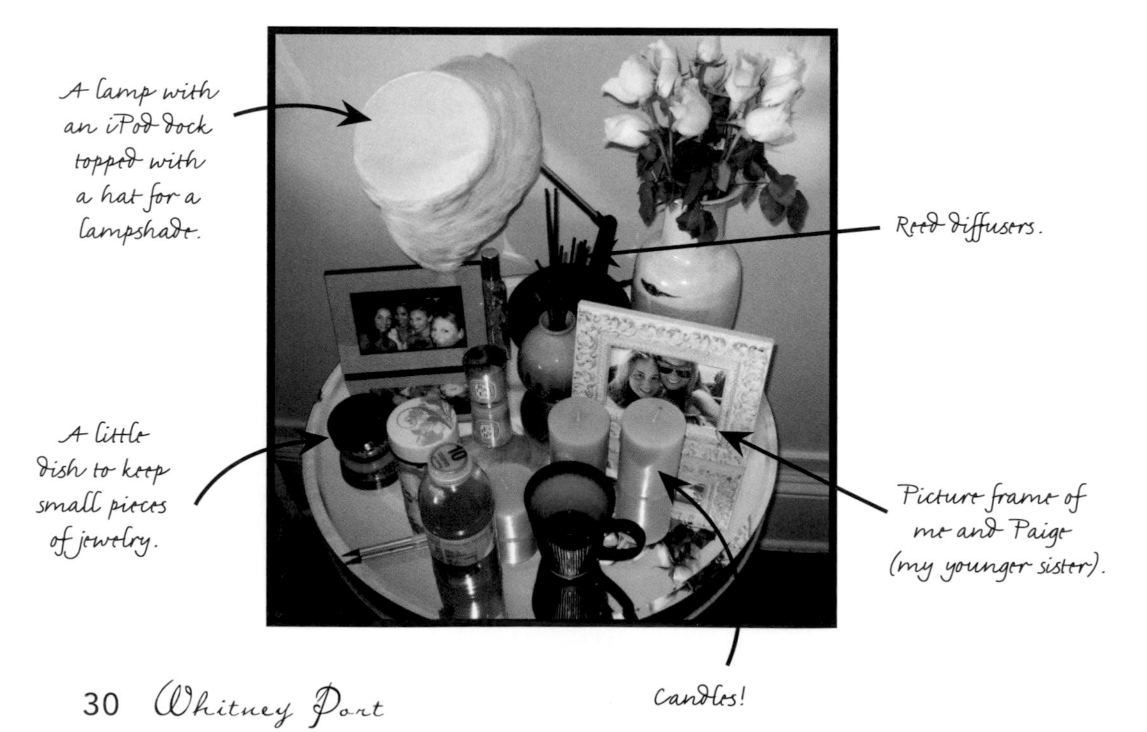

Nightstand Drawer

An essential next to your bed is a good moisturizing hand cream (if you have it handy, you'll use it)—my new fave is called Breathe by Lollia (Lollialife.com), which I found at Anthropologie. You should also have in your nightstand drawer: a condom (if you have it handy, you'll use it!); a good book or your Kindle/iPad; a flashlight; lip moisturizer, makeup-removing towelettes (in case you're too lazy to walk to the bathroom to take off your makeup—it happens to all of us); gum or mints (good as you are putting your purse together to walk out the door) or some gummy candies for late-night snacking; tissues.

Medicine Cabinet

Here you should store your meds (throw out all prescriptions that have expired), Band-Aids in assorted sizes, gauze, antiseptics such as alcohol and hydrogen peroxide for cleansing cuts or scrapes, an antibiotic cream, a salve for minor burns, an anesthetic spray for sunburns, aloe vera, over-the-counter antihistamine for allergic reactions, a cortisone-based topical cream, over-the-counter pain medications, a cough suppressant/expectorant, a cold medication, and a sore throat spray or nose spray for congestion. You might also want to have a sunscreen and a bug spray on hand—especially during the summer—lip balm, tweezers (for eyebrows as well as splinters), and eyedrops.

Bookshelf

Obviously, you should stock your shelves with books you love, even if they're old faves from childhood (Go on! Proudly display your Judy Blume or Nancy Drew collection!), college classics, or just fun, "escape." I keep all of my fashion magazines on my bookshelves—every single issue of *Vogue*, *Bazaar*, and *Elle* since I've been living in NYC. I draw inspiration from them. When I'm stumped on a design or an outfit, or need hairstyle or makeup ideas, I thumb through the pages to revisit fashion seasons past. It's also important to have reference books handy, like a thesaurus and a dictionary, and some books relevant to your job or field (in my case, fashion). And collect a few photo or coffee-table books about beautiful places, people, or things—eye candy that you or your guests can browse.

ON MY SHELVES RIGHT NOW

Are You There, Vodka? It's Me, Chelsea by Chelsea Handler
Chanel and Her World by Edmonde Charles-Roux
Diane: A Signature Life by Diane von Furstenberg
The Fashion Designer Survival Guide by Mary Gehlhar
The Great Gatsby by F. Scott Fitzgerald
If You Have to Cry, Go Outside:
And Other Things Your Mother Never Told You by Kelly Cutrone
Images of Marilyn from Parragon Books
L.A. Candy and *Sweet Little Lies* by Lauren Conrad
Mario Testino: Portraits by Mario Testino
Patrick Demarchelier by Patrick Demarchelier
Poseur by Rachel Maude
Prince of Tides by Pat Conroy
Shabby Chic Interiors by Rachel Ashwell
The *Twilight* Saga by Stephenie Meyer
Valentino: Themes and Variations by Valentino and Pamela Golbin
The Way We Live in the City by Stafford Cliff and Gilles de Chabeneix

Yves Saint Laurent's Style by Foundation Pierre Bergé

DVD Collection

Build a collection of movies from different genres and times, including some tearjerkers, powerhouse dramas, sweeping romances, or even zany comedies. That way, if you have friends over, you have films that appeal to everyone (and you're not scrambling to get to Blockbuster!). I also keep on hand movies that *always* make me laugh and cry or remind me of specific eras in my life (like college or high school). I probably have watched them more than a dozen times each, but I never get tired of them. In fact, I know a lot of the lines by heart: "Isn't my house classic? The columns date all the way back to 1972!" (Alicia Silverstone in *Clueless*).

MY MOVIE MUST-HAVES

Clueless
Elizabethtown
Fast Times at Ridgemont High
Father of the Bride
Forever Young
Forrest Gump
A League of Their Own
Legends of the Fall
Love, Actually
Mermaids
Motorcycle Diaries
My Father the Hero
New York Minute
Now and Then
Pretty Woman
Pursuit of Happyness
Shakespeare in Love
Stand by Me
Teen Witch
When Harry Met Sally

Fridge/Pantry

Basically, you want to cram your kitchen with healthy essentials you will eat every day. For me, that's Granny Smith apples and bananas with freshly churned peanut butter, berries and Reddi-wip, whole-grain English muffins, Parmesan cheese, avocados, almond milk, nonfat Greek yogurt, vegetables to roast, unsalted butter, whole-wheat bread, roasted and unsalted almonds, veggie burgers, cherry tomatoes, Raisin Bran cereal, original Popchips, rice cracker mix, artichokes, plums, and greens. I know other people make and freeze tons of meals ahead of time and their fridges are overflowing with yummy dishes. If you have the time (and the know-how) to cook, that's great. If you're not as culinarily inclined, like me, keep it simple. Make sure you have healthy choices in there that will work for breakfast, lunch, and dinner . . . and everything in between. And keep some backup snack foods on hand in case a friend drops by or you invite a few coworkers back after an event.

A few healthy suggestions (my faves!):

- Fresh vegetables: artichokes, broccoli, cauliflower, brussels sprouts, butternut squash, mushrooms
- Fresh fruit: Granny Smith apples, bananas, papaya, strawberries, pineapple, plums
- Dried fruit: mango, apricots, Craisins
- Frozen fruits: strawberries, blueberries, raspberries
- Salsa: Homemade is always best! I chop tomatoes and onions and add salt, pepper, and a dash of cilantro

- Peanut butter and jelly: My fave PB is fresh churned from Whole Foods
- Almond milk
- Whole grains: bread (love La Brea Bakery bread), pita, brown rice, cereal, healthy crackers, Popchips, red quinoa
- Low-fat microwavable popcorn
- Edamame
- Parmesan chunks with almonds
- Trail mix

Emergency Supplies

Keep these somewhere handy—like a kitchen drawer (not buried in the back of your closet!): a flashlight, batteries, emergency phone numbers, spare set of keys to your home, bottles of water, scissors, screwdrivers (Phillips and flat head) and hammer, candles and matches, transistor radio.

SAFETY SMARTS

Ladies, living alone can be scary—and it goes without saying that you should take a few precautions. In college, I had an experience that creeped me out and taught me something about security. I had this stupid habit of not locking my apartment door. Well, one night, a guy wandered in and got into bed with me! I was freaking out, but tried to sound calm and polite. I said, "Excuse me? Excuse me!" hoping he would take the hint and get out from under my blankets. I later found out he was one of the guys from a neighboring unit. Thankfully, he didn't mean any harm—he just was so wasted, he thought he was in his own bed.

But this unwanted visitor made me think twice about how secure I was in my space. To this day, my mind plays tricks on me. I hear creaking floors and I jump a mile. Probably for this reason, my mom made me get one of those high-tech security systems as well as a second lock. At first, I thought she was being overprotective. But I realize it does help me sleep better at night (my place is locked up tighter than Fort Knox!). I think anytime you're proactive, you feel *much* better. You don't want to be paranoid, but you also don't want to be naive. Here are a few recommendations from the NYPD Crime Prevention Unit that make a lot of sense:

- **If you're coming and going at odd hours** (early in the morning/late at night), and your place doesn't have a doorman or security camera, have someone watch until you get in your door (dates don't seem to mind this . . . it could mean a good-night kiss at the door). Never walk alone past 10:00 P.M.! My mom gets so mad at me if she finds out I was strolling solo past this time. It's like an indirect curfew placed from over three thousand miles away, but it keeps me safe.

- **If you are coming home alone,** double-check that no one is lurking around. Carry your keys in your hand so you can immediately get inside and lock the door behind you. Digging around in the bottom of your bag can allow someone to sneak up behind you. Your keys can also be used as a defensive weapon if someone attacks you. And shut the door right away—do not let it close on its own.

- **Always carry a cell phone!** Carry a personal alarm in your purse. Some come on a key chain and make a loud, piercing sound; others will even dial 911.

- **Avoid places like stairwells,** laundry rooms, and parking lots late at night. There is no reason to be at those places after hours.

- **Make sure the hallway** outside your door is brightly lit. If not, speak to your landlord.

- **Double-check that your windows and doors are locked** securely when you're in and when you're out; you may also want a safety chain or a deadbolt and bars on your windows. The first thing one of my friends bought for her new apartment was a little dog with a big bark! It's like having an alarm system on legs . . .

- **Don't give a lot of people** copies of your keys. And don't leave a spare lying around under your doormat, in a flowerpot, in a mailbox, or in other obvious places. If you tend to lose your keys often, give *one* set to a trusted neighbor or friend.

- **Don't "announce" to everyone that you're a young woman living on your own.** In fact, when you record the message on your home phone, have a guy friend or your dad do it . . . or say "WE can't come to the phone right now . . ." When I moved to NYC, I took my brother's old phone, and his voice still picks up on the answering machine. I've never changed it.

- **Take a woman's personal safety/self-defense class.** It can give you peace of mind, and a lot of police precincts, community colleges, and local Ys offer them for free or for a small fee. Krav Maga is a great one. You'll learn what to watch out for and how to protect yourself in an emergency.

CHAPTER TWO

WORKING GIRL

Job interviews are agonizing enough—try doing one while cameras are filming you! In 2005, I was going to USC and working as an intern at *Women's Wear Daily* in L.A. It was in the same building as *Teen Vogue,* and I heard they were looking for interns as well. I jumped at the opportunity and quickly sent in my résumé. I soon got an invitation to meet with their fashion editorial team. *Gulp.* During the course of the interview, they asked me lots of questions—many of which I was painfully unprepared to answer. I didn't know the names of some of the key editors on staff; I hadn't heard of many of the important photographers they used. I thought I blew it. Then came the strangest question of all, "We've been approached by MTV for a reality TV show. How would you feel about being on camera?"

I didn't really feel anything; I had no idea what this would entail. Seriously . . . I just wanted the job at *Teen Vogue*! I agreed to do a casting tape for MTV, which I thought went a little smoother (they didn't ask me the names of any of *their* staff!). A month later, I was called back to *Teen Vogue*—this time to meet with Lisa Love, the West Coast fashion editor. Don't let her last name fool you; Lisa has a really tough reputation (though she still has a lot of love to give). I knew she would put me to the test. And I was warned that MTV was shooting the whole thing. If I was nervous before, now I was a wreck.

I wanted the job so much I could taste it. It was a great opportunity to make my next move in fashion and *Vogue*—come on, that's the dream! But I also knew I wasn't the only one: when I arrived for the interview, the lobby was filled with eager young hopefuls, all just as qualified—if not more so—as I was. Part of my brain was screaming "Make a run for it!" but I took a deep breath and sunk quietly into a seat. I sat there waiting, waiting, waiting to be called in, and eyeing all the competition.

I wanted the job so much I could taste it.

It was a very formal reception area with a big marble desk, comfy chairs, and big posters of all the current Condé Nast covers. The girls and guys interviewing for a position were all superstylish in sophisticated knee-length skirts or trousers and collared

Where would I be without these ladies? Left, with Rox and Kelly; right, Lauren and me.

Kelly has really helped guide my career and gave me the confidence to follow my designing dreams.

blouses or shirts and ties. None of them seemed to be as jittery as I was. Or maybe they were just better at hiding it.

We chatted and compared experiences, and it made me feel even more insecure; they all seemed so qualified, cool, and confident. Then Lauren Conrad from *Laguna Beach* walked in. Her hair was flat-ironed straight, and she was wearing a tailored blouse, a dark pencil skirt, and high heels. The girl looked so put together and professional (even though I later learned she had ten minutes to change and get down there!). How would I stand a chance against *her*? I looked down at my outfit. I *thought* I looked cute when I left the house: I was wearing a vintage collared beige blouse and *jeans*. What was I thinking? And as if that wasn't bad enough, I rounded out the outfit with Frye boots. Yikes! But I was holding in my hands a printed résumé when a lot of the girls and guys didn't have theirs—so hopefully that earned me brownie points for being prepared.

Lucky for me, Lisa Love and the rest of the staff at *Teen Vogue* saw beyond my bad fashion choices. I think my passion and drive to learn convinced them I wasn't a total disaster. I got the job, and Lauren (she was also hired as a fashion department intern) and I, of course, became good friends. But I learned a lot about what to do—and not to do—on an interview and in the workplace.

THE JOB INTERVIEW

So here's the good news: if you're called for an interview, the employer thinks you potentially have what it takes. You look great on paper; now comes your chance to show what you've got and prove you're as fabulous as your cover letter claims. The goal of the interview is not just to see if you're the real deal; it's also to evaluate if you and the company "mesh." The interviewer wants to make sure you're a good fit to work here. You want to be yourself in any interview, but you also want to show that you are capable of adapting to any work environment with enthusiasm, that you will have respect for your fellow staffers, and that you possess ingenuity. Every workplace is unique, and of course, it's the sum of its parts. It's the people who make up the company as much as it is the product/service that's offered. So the interviewer needs to see that you're going to be comfortable and make those around you comfortable as well.

Put on a happy face.

Seriously. Do not come in looking like you've just lost your best friend or your cell phone on the bus. Worry shows; wipe it from your face and flash a dazzling smile as you firmly shake the interviewer's hand (I did say firm; not a vicelike grip!). A handshake is underrated. My dad has judged many a man who has walked through our front door based on his grip! Tell yourself you're going to be positive and optimistic; practice thinking happy thoughts: "I will get this job. I am a great catch for any company!" So when you walk in and see that interviewer for the first time, you project confidence, charisma, and a coolness that only someone sincerely wonderful could possess. This is not faking it; this is making it happen!

Follow his/her lead.

If the interviewer engages in small talk ("Crazy weather we're having!" "Love your shoes!"), then by all means relax and chat right back. Be appropriate, yes, but also realize he/she may be trying to put you at ease or gauge how much of a "people person" you are. If your answers are only monosyllabic, you won't allow the interviewer to get a feel for how you communicate. Expect the unexpected. A friend of mine went into a serious interview at an investment bank, expecting to be quizzed about the state of the economy and Wall Street. Instead, the interviewer wanted to know (since my friend mentioned on her résumé she had briefly studied in Italy) if she had been to Voltera where they shot the *New Moon* movie. They spent an hour gabbing about their mutual passion for *Twilight* and RPattz; not a word about finance was uttered. And guess what? She got the job on the spot!

Then there was Roxy. I know she might have come off a little abrasive in her interview with notoriously tough Kelly Cutrone at People's Revolution, but really, she was riffing off Kelly's vibe. Pretty ingenious: she was trying to show Kelly she was a lot like her (attitude and all!).

Tell yourself you're going to be positive and optimistic. This is not faking it; this is making it happen!

Make yourself perfectly clear.

That means make sure you say what you mean and that you speak loud enough and articulate (no mumbling!) so the interviewer understands you. Think before you open your mouth; listen carefully to what he/she has just asked you. If you don't understand the question, ask the interviewer to repeat it ("Excuse me? Can you repeat that?"). Or better yet, say the question in your own words and ask the interviewer to confirm that you understood properly. I'm not afraid to say, "That's a really difficult question . . ." and then take a deep breath and think it through. I try not to blurt something out without processing it.

Sometimes an interviewer might even say something you don't agree with. When this happens to me, I try to be rational and levelheaded. My mom always told me to validate someone's feelings, then in a polite way state my opinion. So I'll say "I hear you" or "Fair enough," then explain my take on it. Sometimes people respect when their authority is questioned and you prove you have a strong viewpoint.

What if you're still stumped? Think about what the interviewer would want/expect you to say—and what the *true* purpose of the question is. For example, on an interview at Bergdorf's when I was showing my clothing line, the buyer asked me what I thought of a certain fabric on one of my samples. I loved this fabric, but I could tell she was fishing for something (and potentially hated it). So I explained why I thought it was the perfect material for a dress: comfy, forgiving of any figure flaws, and it had a touch of sparkle to it, which made it ideal for transforming quickly from a day to evening look. She was satisfied with my response, even if she didn't flip over my fabric choice. Why? Because I allowed her to see my thought process when creating my line. Her question really had a secret underlying question: "Whitney, how do you design?"

Ask away!

The best way to convey you're eager to join the team (without getting up on the desk and doing a cheer) is to ask relevant and intelligent questions. I'm not talking about "So how long do we get for lunch?" or "What's your policy on sick days?" or even "Do we get year-end bonuses?" or "Is there a free dress day?" Even if these questions are burning in your mind, stick to the topics you know the interviewer would like to hear about: "What is the company's goal for the upcoming year?" "What would my role be and what would a typical day be like for me?" As you leave, give the interviewer a firm handshake and thank him/her for meeting with you. Make sure to show a lot of interest in the company—people love curiosity.

IT'S ALL IN THE FOLLOW-THROUGH

Always ask for a business card. You'll want to follow up (and not misspell the interviewer's name!) with a thank-you note or e-mail. Do it right away; don't wait a week to drop a line saying, "Thanks for meeting with me!" Remind the interviewer (who has probably seen several other candidates for the position) that you are very interested, excited, and ready to come work for them. Don't beg . . . just enthusiastically communicate how much you enjoyed hearing about the company and are confident you would be a benefit to the organization, even suggest new ideas or projects—this shows a proactive nature. I remember stopping in repeatedly at this store named Sara's in Santa Monica where I had applied for a job as a holiday gift wrapper. I was relentless; I wouldn't stop bugging them until they told me when my first day was. I desperately wanted to make some extra cash over the holidays, and I knew that if I was persistent, I would wear them out. Of course, I was a quirky fourteen-year-old at the time—I do not recommend stalking an employer if you're twenty-four! But you get the point: a gentle reminder (or in my case a not-so-gentle one) can work wonders.

When I interviewed at DVF, I *immediately* e-mailed Alixe Boyer (my future boss!) to communicate how serious I was about this job.

WHIT 101: INTERVIEW DOS AND DON'TS

- **DO** know where you're going. Have the exact address, and if you're not sure, make a practice run via train, bus, or car. Getting lost is not an option: it will make you late and stressed out. Late is unacceptable!

- **DO** your homework. Research the company, what it does, recent press, and so on. Know the names of the key players (CEO, editor in chief, etc.).

- **DO** practice what you will say in the interview. Have a friend role-play with you—and even throw you some curveball questions. You'll feel perfectly prepared.

- **DO** dress the part. If you're in a creative field, you can probably get away with more. But always be a bit conservative. Save the bold accents for a single accessory (remember the girl in the green scarf in *Confessions of a Shopaholic*?). You want to be memorable, yes, not laughable.

- **DO** get to the interview at least fifteen minutes early. And if you're stuck in traffic and can't possibly be there on time, call the company and give them a heads-up.

- **DO** treat the receptionist or assistant with courtesy. The person you interview with may ask their opinion of you!

- **DO** use mouthwash, or have a mint immediately before the interview, plus a little spritz of perfume.

- **DO** check yourself in a compact mirror or the bathroom mirror to make sure there are no lipstick smudges on or spinach caught between your teeth. Or boogers! Or eye boogers!

- **DO** bring extra résumés to the interview—and a portfolio of your work if it's relevant.

- **DO** greet the interviewer with a firm handshake and a smile. Make eye contact throughout the whole interview and show you're confident. First impressions count!

- **DO** address the interviewer by his or her formal name: Mr. or Mrs. or Dr. _____. And if you're not sure how to pronounce the name, ask the receptionist. Don't mangle it!

- **DON'T** chew gum during the interview.

- **DON'T** make inappropriate jokes ("Did you hear the one about the editor and the call girl?")

- **DON'T** beg for the job or act desperate . . . even if you are.

- **DON'T** say negative things about your former employers ("My old boss was a total psycho!"). Rox almost blew her interview with Kelly when she bad-mouthed her former colleagues. It makes an employer question whether you're really a team player.

- **DON'T** say negative things about yourself ("I'm such a klutz! I'm so forgetful!"). Self-deprecating humor will not win over an employer. If you are unsure about yourself, then they will be, too.

- **DON'T** lie. Ever. It will come back to bite you in the butt, I promise. Someone, somewhere will find out. Answer questions truthfully, and don't exaggerate your experience.

- **DON'T** answer questions with a simple yes or no. Elaborate and explain. Give examples.

- **DON'T** bring up personal or family problems. Your future employer doesn't care if you just broke up with your boyfriend. Too much information . . .

- **DON'T** answer your cell phone during the interview. Turn off your phone; the interview is the most important thing and nothing should distract you from it.

DRESS TO IMPRESS: YOUR FIRST-DAY OUTFIT

My first day at DVF, I wore a yellow patterned dress with patent leather coral-colored heels. I thought I looked the part of a stylish DVF representative, and my ensemble stood out enough but not *too* much. It also made me feel bright, sunny, and optimistic—and I hoped that was what I conveyed to my coworkers. But I'm comfy in color; someone else might feel more confident in a figure-flattering black dress. Dressing for a job is different from dressing for everyday occasions. You are not just taking into account your own style and taste, but also what's "appropriate" in the workplace. So while your fave uniform might be jeans and a hoodie, that attire simply doesn't work for work (unless your workplace is the Gap). In fact, once you land your first job, you'll probably need to go shopping for some work basics that you can mix and match. I made sure I had lots of pairs of black tights, suit jackets, belts, comfortable pumps, and *really* big purses (to carry shoes, a laptop, my iPod, makeup bag, lunch, not to mention wallet, keys, and sunglasses/glasses. *Phew*!).

Sometimes it's really hard to know what to wear to work—especially when you're starting a new job. Most companies will not present you with a strict dress code; they trust you'll look around, see what goes, and strive to fit in. In general, you want to opt for a mix of professionalism and sophisticated fashion. You want to feel comfortable (especially if you're on your feet a lot) but also look polished. It's a good idea to look around when you go for the interview; make a mental note of what the women are wearing. But if you didn't—or if you forgot—just think simple and conservative. It's hard to go wrong with a pretty blouse and a black skirt.

Just a few things to keep in mind (I hope these go without saying . . . but I gotta say them):

- No cleavage.
- No microminis.
- No Moon Boots or sky-high platforms.
- No skintight leather.
- No going commando; undies are a must!
- No ripped, tattered, or stained clothing (even if you've patched it).
- No bra straps, panty lines, or belly-button piercings on display.
- No tees with offensive slogans. Roxy recently wore a shirt to *Glamour*'s offices that said the "F" word. The editors were in shock (and I was a little embarrassed)!

A pencil skirt is a sophisticated cut, but this fabric is metallic and playful.

This outfit is demure but still fashion-forward with purffy sleeves and stripes. It mixes edge with femininity.

I also caution you to beware of overdoing makeup and perfume; your cubicle mate might not appreciate being choked by Chanel No. 5. And you want your face to look pretty—not pageanty. No spidery false eyelashes, rag-doll rouge, or Angelina-like lips (unless they're naturally yours). If you're having a beauty treatment (or trying one out on yourself), make sure you do so at least a week before you start work so you can fix it if it fails. Ya never know . . . I once spray-tanned the day before starting my job at *WWD* and was so embarrassed by how orangey and blotchy I was! I haven't done it since. Sometimes first impressions are just unfortunate and unfair. Try your hardest not to overdo makeup for work. Think less is more!

LAUREN CONRAD'S ADVICE FOR GETTING ALONG AT THE OFFICE

Lauren Conrad was the coolest co-worker at *Teen Vogue*—not to mention a great, loyal friend. She's the kind of person you wished shared the cubicle next to yours! Here are her tips on how to succeed on your first go-round in the workplace:

Do your job.

If you are given a job, do it, and do it in a timely manner. Don't expect others to pick up your slack. And if your boss asks you to do something *not* in your job description (but within reason), rise to the occasion. While we were working for *Teen Vogue,* Whit was asked to step in, not once, but twice for missing models. Not only was Whit a great employee, but she also towered over the other interns and looked like a model herself. I'll never forget watching her walk the runway in the DKNY Jeans show. It was her first time, and she rocked it!

Play nice.

The workplace doesn't always have to be about competition. You are there every day, so it's much more enjoyable if it's a friendly environment.

Respect others.

You may have a higher job title or a larger desk, but working in an office is all about teamwork. Everyone's job is an important part of the puzzle, so be sure to give them all the respect they deserve. Also, a thank-you goes a long way.

Bring treats.

Whether it's Valentine sweets or baked goods, it's nice to bring in a little something special every once in a while. Just be sure to bring enough to go around.

Be punctual.

We're all late occasionally, but try not to make it a habit. It's unprofessional, especially if you are working as a group. Don't make others pay because you hit the snooze button.

Don't overshare.

It's great to have friends in the workplace, but it's still the workplace. Save the juicy stuff for after-work drinks or get-togethers outside of the office.

Steer clear of gossip.

The workplace, no matter what size, is a small place. Gossip travels quickly and it can be pretty unpleasant to work with someone who has been saying negative things about you, and vice versa.

Curb your complaints.

Everyone has a job they hate at some point. It's up to you to decide what kind of attitude you are going to have about it. There's nothing worse than working with someone who hates his or her job—and lets everyone know.

Lauren was such an incomparable coworker—and is also one of my closest friends!

MY SPACE

Some people just love to embellish . . . everything. That includes their office space, even if it's itty-bitty and out in the open for all to see. I remember walking into DVF and seeing a rhinestone-studded stapler and tape dispenser on Olivia Palermo's desk sitting next to a vase brimming with roses. Hmmm . . . a bit over the top, I thought (more power to her though). I feel that your work space should be clean, uncluttered, and free from fussiness that could distract not just you but your fellow workers. A few simple photos in small frames (as long as they're not of you and your guy in a hot tub), a favorite mug, a paperweight from your alma mater . . . all okay. But since witnessing Olivia's adorned desk I have steered clear of most decorations. I tend to keep my personal office space neat and organized with not too many trimmings. Honestly, we have so little space at People's Revolution, there is no room for fuss!

And remember that your office computer is not for your personal use. That means no screensavers of your party days, no IMing your roommate, no following your Facebook groups. These are the things that drive bosses crazy.

You should also be wary that the walls have ears. Literally. People love to eavesdrop. Even if you think you're being discreet when calling your ob-gyn from your cube, chances are everyone around you is getting an earful. Save the steamy conversations with your boyfriend and the blowouts with your best friend for after work and at home. Some of your officemates will be offended, while others will love listening to (and gossiping about) your little life dramas.

EATING ON THE JOB

Part of succeeding at work is making sure you have the tools you need—and that includes the right snacks to stay focused and healthy. When you feel the

midday brain drain, scarfing down some candy from the vending machine—or making a run to the coffee store for an iced mocha something—sounds very tempting. When you're tired and stressed at work, it's hard to resist a little pick-me-up. Sugar and caffeine offer instant gratification. But guess what? Less than an hour later, the euphoria has worn off, and you're even more tired than before.

There are smart ways to snack. When I know I am going to have a busy day—and have no idea where or when my next meal will be—I pack a bunch of snacks such as fruit leather, dried fruit, or a banana. I slice a Granny Smith apple and put a spoonful of peanut butter in a Tupperware container. Or I pack a baggie of popcorn to pop in the office micro, a handful of almonds, maybe a Fiber One bar and a Vitaminwater. It's a good idea to eat something that contains both protein and carbs; this will help maintain your blood-sugar level for the rest of the afternoon and stave off your hunger until the next meal. Some other good snacks to keep handy:

Nuts.
They provide healthy fats along with fiber—so you stay fuller longer. Buy a bunch of different unsalted varieties and make your own trail mix.

Hummus.

This is a low-glycemic-index food. Translation: These foods release their energy slowly, so you won't feel that dreaded blood-sugar spike after you refuel. Try two table-spoons of hummus with ten baby carrots. It's only about a hundred calories!

A sweet potato.

Pop one in the microwave and you'll instantly erase your sugar craving (and fill up on fiber). Fill with a little salt, pepper, olive oil, and Girard's light champagne dressing.

Edamame.

Soy beans are a vegetable loaded with protein. Microwave them, add a little salt, and you're set. Pair them with some Wheat Thins and you're good to go!

DAY TO NIGHT: HOW TO TRANSFORM YOUR WORK ATTIRE TO ON-THE-TOWN CHIC

Some days you are *so* busy, you just won't have the opportunity to go home and change before going out. This happens to me all the time, so I've become quite the "quick-change artist." I can get ready for a date or a girls' night out with lightning speed. It's simple: I either add to or take off from my day look.

Here's how:

Start with a little black dress in silk, satin, velvet, chiffon, or even jersey knit.

The posh material screams "party." But when you wear it to work, topped with a simple blazer or cardigan, it's suddenly office appropriate. When it's time to go out, peel off the jacket or sweater and you're ready!

Accessorize!

The fastest way to dress up a simple sheath or suit is to add beautiful jewelry. I pile on bangles, chains, dangly earrings (you can store them in a zip bag in your purse). Or carry a glitzy evening bag or clutch (just tuck it in your tote). The touch of sparkle makes your outfit evening-ready instantly.

Swap your shoes.

Leave the loafers under your desk. A pair of sexy stilettos or ankle boots glams up even the most mundane office attire. I especially like to strap on a pair in gold or silver—or a bold color. Very flirty!

Change your do.

If you normally wear your hair up at the office, then let it down at night. Or if you like it loose for day, sweep it into a messy bun for evening. The idea is to do your do differently. You'll feel special and sexy. And confidence is the best accessory!

Makeup makeover.

Bring makeup remover towelettes and remove face makeup, then put on some tinted moisturizer, blush, and bronzer for an instant glow. Slick on a darker, more daring lipstick and smoky eyeliner for evening. They'll instantly make your face look more glam and refreshed. These wipes can double to wipe under your armpits. Always carry a little stick of deodorant to reapply. Don't forget to spritz on a little perfume, too. Scent invigorates!

WHITTYISM: HOW TO HIDE A HANGOVER AT WORK

One of the best parts of being a single gal in the city is staying out late (no curfews!) and partying with friends. The worst part: waking up on a weekday morning after I've danced till dawn and downed one too many glasses of champagne. Luckily, I've found a way to erase the effects of a hangover from hell before I hit the office! (Or at least I try.)

When You Get Home

- Always wash your face before going to bed or use Pond's, L'Oreal, or Comodynes Wet Cleansing Towelettes.
- Even if your head is pounding, try to brush your hair before going to bed. It will feel so good on your scalp! And even rub in some Moroccan oil as a conditioning agent.
- Run some Frédéric Fekkai Protein Rx Creme through your tresses, then twist them into a bun. You'll wake to pretty waves and volume.
- Smooth on eye cream and lip balm, and lots of face moisturizer.
- Chug water!

In the A.M.

- Drinking takes its toll on skin; alcohol will dry your face out like the Sahara. So spritz skin with a moisturizing spray (or in a pinch, plain, cool water) to give it a freshening wake-up call. Finer Skin Institute and Philosophy make great ones.
- Apply a rich, soothing moisturizer—preferably one with some built-in shimmer, like Fresh High Noon Freshface Glow tinted moisturizer—to brighten and replenish.
- Next, focus on the eyes—they're probably swollen, ringed with dark circles, and bloodshot. Rohto cooling eyedrops will instantly get the red out, and a soothing eye cream (look for ones that specifically cool and firm) is a must before applying concealer—otherwise known as a girl's best friend. I also put spoons in the freezer and then rest the backs of the spoons on my eyelids for fifteen minutes. Ahh . . . It really works!
- Finally, bring the glow back to your cheeks with a dot of rosy blush and bronzer such as Nars Orgasm and Nars Laguna. You want to add just a hint of color to your complexion—especially if you look green or pasty. Don't overdo it–a dead giveaway that you were out all night and are trying to hide the evidence.

EVIL COWORKERS

Honey, it happens . . . you suddenly realize you're being asked to work alongside Cruella De Vil. These toxic types abound in the workplace. I was shocked when at DVF, my colleague Olivia Palermo went from palling around to plotting against me in a matter of weeks. At first, I thought she was just a shallow society girl—haughty but harmless. I had a hunch that the producers picked her for *The City* because she was very outspoken; I didn't suspect she was also underhanded. When we were assigned to pull DVF clothes together for an upcoming Jessica Alba shoot, she was bossy and opinionated. She trashed every outfit I suggested and allowed only one—a cute floral jacket and shorts—to make it to the rack for the shoot. When my outfit was actually chosen for the cover, Olivia quickly took all the credit. I stood there, utterly dumbfounded as my boss, Alixe, patted her on the back, and Olivia, who was beaming, said, "Styling is my passion!"

In retrospect, I was just as much to blame as she was. I didn't speak up when my boss congratulated her for spearheading the project. I allowed myself to be a doormat. What was I thinking? I knew I had chosen that outfit, but I didn't take credit where credit was due. I didn't try to set the record straight. I guess I was a little intimidated—but also just utterly stunned that someone could be so ruthless. I am also someone who doesn't like conflict; I hate to make a scene. But in situations like this, when someone you work with is clearly lying, cheating, and trying to make you look like a loser, you have to stand up for yourself! I vented to my girlfriends about it—which made me feel better—but then I simply stood there *again* at a luncheon with Diane von Furstenberg and Joe Zee, the creative director of *Elle,* as Olivia told them all, "I pulled that look!" Such a lie!

Every time I tried to work with Olivia, it was the same story: she was dismissive, rolled her eyes, and acted as if I was an idiot when it came to fashion. What was *that* about? Well, it was meant to knock my confidence for a loop. I totally see that now: when someone is insecure about her own abilities, she tries to put you down to make herself feel bigger and better. Classic bully technique.

Of course—as anyone who's ever seen a Disney cartoon knows—the villain eventually gets her just deserts. I say *eventually,* because it may not happen for a long, long time and you may begin to think there is no justice in the universe! When we were doing a presentation of DVF handbags, I was a nervous wreck, and Olivia kept telling me she wasn't worried at all ("Easy! Piece of cake!"). Then she totally stuttered and stammered and lost it at the presentation. Redemption!

With Olivia Palermo at Bryant Park—I'm too excited for the Diane von Furstenberg show to worry about our dysfunctional relationship.

Even though we don't work together anymore, Olivia still knows how to push my buttons. She is now a journalist for Elle.com and she interviews up-and-coming designers (that would be me!). So we scheduled a photo shoot for the site, and she was all set to come and interview me about my Whitney Eve line. Well, true to form, she decided three hours into the shoot that she wasn't coming because she didn't want to "endorse" my line. She kept saying that she had personal issues she had to deal with, but I didn't buy it. It felt like once again, she was trying to put me down and make me look bad.

> I *so* wanted to tell her what I thought of her manipulative and mean-spirited tactics!

But did I let Olivia irritate me all over again? Well, maybe for a few minutes . . . but then I shrugged it off. When you have a coworker who gets on your nerves, you have to rise above. Do your best. Work your hardest. If you get caught up in all the toxic talk and mind games, you're going to wind up making *yourself* look bad (something she is trying so hard to do!). I *so* wanted to tell her what I thought of her manipulative and mean-spirited tactics! I wanted to shout, "Olivia, what is your problem?" or rat her out to our bosses. But my friends told me not to sink to her level, to not get caught up in the drama. Instead, they told me to just focus, be myself, be the bigger person. I think that's great advice. Eventually, in a very peaceful manner, I did give her a piece of my mind, but it served more as closure for me than as a lesson for her.

Here's some other ways to deal with divas at work:

Keep your cool.

As tempting as it may be to launch into a tirade (or give her the good spanking she deserves), remember you are in a professional workplace. You have to behave like a pro. Let her be the one to make a scene; try to keep cool, no matter how many buttons she pushes. One of my friends told me when she gets worked up at work, she pictures Glinda the Good Fairy from *The Wizard of Oz* leaning over her shoulder, waving her twinkling wand, and ridding the room of that wicked witch. Try it; you may just giggle at the thought, but it certainly will take your mind off the tension.

Don't share your personal biz.

When I was breaking up with Jay Lyon, I was really sad. Olivia asked me (pretending to be concerned) why I seemed so down. When I told her, she snapped, "You need to focus on your work, not your relationship. Don't bring him into the workplace. That's incredibly immature." So much for sympathy! But I laid myself open to it; I should *never* have shared private info with someone I know has it out for me.

Stay away from a showdown.

Olivia loved to lure me in to one-upmanship . . . like the time we went to meet Manolo Blahnik at Bergdorf's. I was so excited to be buying my first pair, and Olivia announced she not only owned several, but had since she was seventeen! Well, I couldn't top that one and I wasn't going to let her ruin my excitement. Instead of trying to one-up her, I just thought: *Okay, Olivia, you win.* It's a waste of energy to get into a game of "Anything you can do, I can do better." You can't waste your time constantly defending yourself to people who only try to bring you down because of their own insecurities.

CHAPTER THREE

STYLE

Part of becoming your own person is developing and owning your personal style. I like to think of it as getting into your fashion groove: what looks good; what feels good; what colors and styles are superflattering to your body and skin tone. It's all about *you*. If everyone wore the same style, we'd all look like those cookie-cutter chicks in the Robert Palmer videos. No two people are exactly alike, and your style should be as unique as you are.

But fashion can be intimidating: all those crazy couture looks on the runway, all the new trends and fads being touted in the fashion magazines. How do you know which ones will work for you—and which will make you look like Lady Gaga? How do you know what to buy and what you can even afford? When you're this confused and overwhelmed, it's much easier to just pull on the same pair of jeans and sneakers and call it a day. Like most subjects, style requires some study. Yes, you're out of college, but you still have some homework ahead of you.

Start with a stack of fashion magazines, like *Vogue, Elle, Harper's Bazaar, Glamour,* or *InStyle*. As you look at photos or ads, what colors catch your eye? What styles can you see yourself wearing with confidence? Don't get hung up on the fact that the people wearing these clothes may be thinner/taller/more endowed than you are. Trust me; few people in real life look like they regularly strut the catwalks.

If you love something, there is *always* a way to wear it. I draw inspiration from style.com, where I can watch all the runway shows and how each look is styled. It's a great way to gauge what's "in fashion" and also figure out how everything works together. Another great site that sparks my creativity is whowhatwear.com.

> If you love something, there is *always* a way to wear it.

Once you've done a little homework, start by pulling a few pieces out of your closet and putting them together in a way that gels with your new "vision." Maybe it's pairing a bold-colored accessory—like a belt, a hat, a bag, or shoes—with a neutral classic. Maybe it's mixing superfeminine pieces—like lacy camisoles or silky blouses—with something more casual, like jeans or even leather. Consider this: What do you want your style to say about you? It can be anything from "I'm sophisticated and elegant" to "I'm funky and fun-loving." And don't think that you have to stick with this style if you suddenly feel inspired to change it. I am a bit of a fashion schizophrenic; I don't ever become married to one look for too long. It's more fun that way!

Inspiration board for Whitney Eve.

My messy closet!

MY FASHION EVOLUTION

Although I love Valentino and Zac Posen, I think my favorite fashion designer is my grandma Bucka. When I was little, she would design intricate clothes for my Corolle baby doll (I didn't want my baby to be a girl, so I named her Michael!). Well, thanks to Bucka, Michael had stunning ensembles: matching tops and bottoms with pretty buttons and fancy ribbons; chic matching hats. My baby was always the best dressed on the block.

Family has always been a huge influence on my fashion taste. My mom is an art teacher, so her love of color definitely rubbed off on me. In fact, in my yearbook, it says "Whitney Port: Most Likely to . . . invent her own highlighter color." But the rest of my style, that's all my own. I have never been one to conform. From the time I was old enough to dress myself, I liked to push the envelope in a tasteful, fun way. My fashion staples when I was a teen were lived-in Hard Tail sweats, UGG boots, checkered Vans, jean jackets, and anything rhinestoned. Then I got turned on to lingerie—but I couldn't keep it covered up! When I was thirteen, I was invited to bar and bat mitzvahs where most girls loved to step out in elegant evening dresses. What I wore to the parties were pieces of lingerie from Only Hearts. I wasn't channeling Madonna; I just had no chest, so the silky slips fit well and were comfy and looked ultrafeminine. I'd sometimes even pick up a lacy tank and silk pj bottoms and wear them as an outfit. I remember wearing a velvet snake-

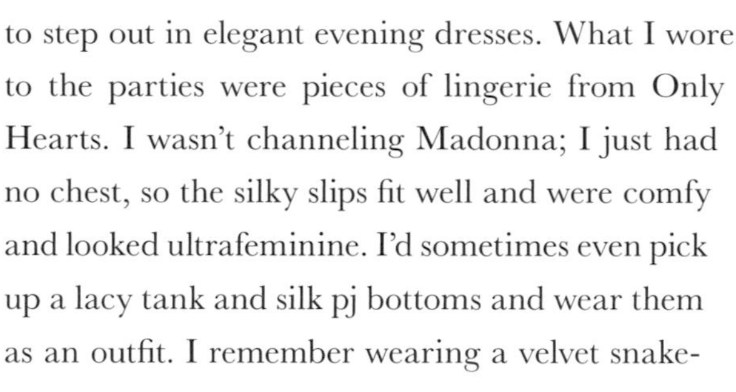

Family has always been a huge influence on my fashion taste.

skin skirt and top with lace edging to my best friend's bat mitzvah. I can't believe my parents let me walk out the door like that! When girls wore fancy dresses to the high school semiformal, I wore a turquoise lace crop top with butterflies and rhinestones. Yes, you could say I liked to make an entrance.

Lover of fashion for as long as I can remember. (Mama has some good taste as well—she dressed us.)

My style has evolved based on my job and my location. When I was in high school, I was very carefree. But I didn't make fashion a huge priority. I'm a jeans and T-shirt girl. In high school, it was relaxed: Hard Tail or Juicy sweats and UGG boots were my uniform. In college at USC when I was in L.A., my look was a lot more California girl—I wore cowboy boots and little fun flirty dresses that were definitely more revealing. Then as I got into fashion, I started to follow designers and trends more. I never really cared about labels, but now I like to mix and match high and low end. Today, my go-to style is some sort of high-waisted, glitzy skirt with a tee tucked in, a blazer on top, and a pair of ankle boots. I pay more at-

I love mixing patterns and textures. Matching is too boring for me!

tention now to the complete look as opposed to just throwing separates together.

When filming *The City,* I rarely wear the same thing twice. As fun as that sounds, it's not easy, especially because I have no budget for clothes or even a stylist on set. It's all up to me, which is why I just recently hired my own stylist, Lara Backmender, to help me pull looks together when I'm crazy busy. And now that I'm a designer, I can wear my own line whenever I want, wherever I want. I love to show off my designs and represent the line.

So from Hard Tails to YSL, I have certainly redefined my fashion philosophy over the years. I realized that by putting just a little more effort into choosing an outfit and thinking outside the box, and outside of what's easiest, I can express myself in my clothes. Sometimes my outfits will earn raves, and other times they elicit some pretty puzzled looks, but I don't care either way. For me, fashion is about being inventive and creative; it's playing with color, cut, texture, and pattern, and mixing them up or blending them to achieve something fresh, new, and exciting. It's an art form. My fashion rule of thumb is simple: be who you are. If you were to ask me to explain my style, I'd have to say "contemporary funk mixed with classic femininity." Translation: it's hard to put a label on my look, and I like it that way.

Whitney, you say, this may work for you. But how can I march to my own fashion drummer and look polished and stylish? Here's the thing: you have to take a few risks. You can't be worried about what someone will think. That said, I wouldn't tell you to wear a bikini and sarong to a black-tie event (unless the theme was Hawaiian Luau!). But you could wear a sexy splash of floral print and liven up that stuffy room.

The idea is to interpret fashion so that it works for you. Think of it as putting your own special spin on an outfit—like I did with those formal-looks-gone-funky for my dances. I "Whitneyfy" my outfit each day to incorporate styles from all differ-

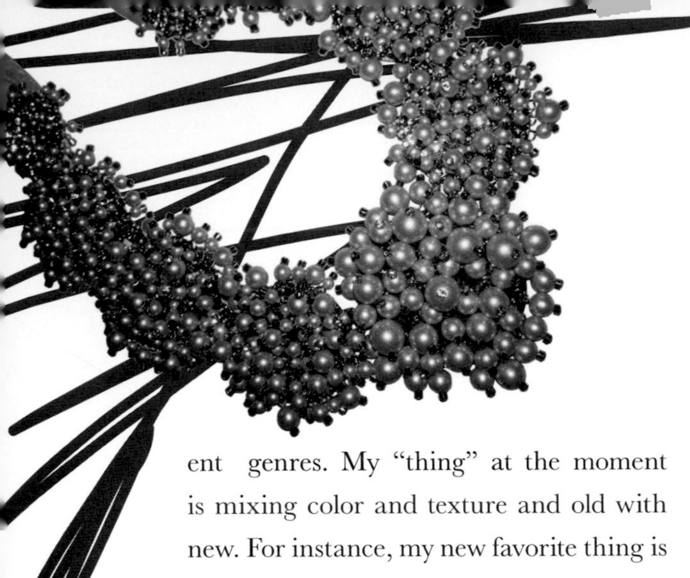

ent genres. My "thing" at the moment is mixing color and texture and old with new. For instance, my new favorite thing is to wear textured tights with silk shorts and vintage sweaters. Add a pair of snakeskin pumps and some bold costume jewelry and I'm all set!

Maybe this look isn't exactly your style; that's fine. You should never copy what someone is wearing just because they're wearing it. And what's trendy today may not be right for you. If it's not something you'd feel comfortable in—but you like *some* part of the look—then do it your way. And no one expects you to get it right every day; where would the world (and the celebrity weeklies!) be without fashion faux pas? I have had my share. I remember wearing a red minidress with black dots all over it, paired with a black braided belt with black stockings and ankle boots, to *The Hills* Season 2 premiere party at Area in Hollywood. The whole cast was there, and I thought I looked cute when I left the house. But when I saw myself in photos . . . yikes. I looked like a giant ladybug! I was a complete fashion nightmare. To top it off, I had these horrible Curly Sue ringlets all over my head. So Shirley Temple meets Ladybug. Hands down one of the worst outfits I've ever worn.

The key is to fill your wardrobe with clothes that work together effortlessly.

I am also not always a fountain of fashion ideas. Trust me; there are many mornings where I rip through my closet and want to wave a white flag in surrender. I can't find a thing to wear. Nada. Nothing fits, matches, or is clean/unwrinkled or remotely cute. Sound familiar? I keep a binder

Me at age seven, with my sister Paige, age five. Even at a young age I took fashion risks and wore highlighter-colored leopard-print outfits!

of torn-out fashion magazine spreads that I like, and sometimes I will try to emulate outfits from those shoots with my own clothes. The key is to fill your wardrobe with clothes that work together effortlessly (see the section "The Basics: Building Your Style" on p. 78), and you'll have less outfit agita. The way you achieve "style" is to build upon those basics. As you get more adept at fashion, you'll develop a "sixth sense" for what works together and what works for you. Picking out an outfit the night before also saves a lot of time and energy. In high school, I used to lay out my outfits on the floor from top to bottom, with accessories and all.

WHO IS YOUR STYLE ICON?

When you're exploring your fashion personality, it helps to have a frame of reference. Who are the actors/personalities who embody your style philosophy? Are you an Elle Woods . . . or a Jackie O? Would you kill for Sarah Jessica Parker's style or do you prefer Posh Spice? The point is not to copy your style crush completely; instead, use her as a role model for what you're trying to achieve, be it sophistication and elegance (Audrey Hepburn, Cate Blanchett), boho chic (Kate Hudson, Keira Knightley, Ashley Olsen), or even rebel rocker (Rihanna, Kate Moss). Study what these women do with their ensembles: how they pair things together, accessorize, emphasize certain features. Then when you're putting together your own looks, channel your style icon's vibe. I have a huge list of icons, both old and new—but here are a few of my all-time faves:

Princess Diana

Shy Di (remember the high-necked frilly blouses?) transformed herself into the epitome of a powerful '90s woman. Her gowns were sleek and showed off her incredible legs and strong shoulders. She also embraced color (one of her favorites was bright red) and was the first in the royal family to be photographed both in jeans and a bikini! She took the stuffiness out of royal dressing and showed the world how to look and act like a modern girl!

Bianca Jagger

The woman was married to Mick, palled around with Warhol, and was Halston's muse. Need I say more? She truly embodied the image of fun-loving party girl back in the '70s disco age (who else would have the guts to ride a white horse into her thirtieth birthday bash at Studio 54?). I love that she has always taken fashion risks: her wedding gown had a deep, plunging neckline (so much for blushing bride!), and to this day she experiments with color, pattern, texture. She's even raided the men's department. Because she has such confidence in her style, she makes even the most over-the-top outfit the envy of everyone in the room.

Brigitte Bardot

The beautiful French actress was the essence of ooh-la-la sexy in the '60s; she's credited for making the bikini popular and for turning "bed head" into a hairstyle! She projected "sex kitten" no matter what she wore, although *j' adore* her pencil skirts and figure-hugging dresses with that French attention to flirty detail.

Faye Dunaway

What a fabulous femme fatale! As the gun-toting gangster moll in *Bonnie and Clyde,* she strutted confidently in slim tailored skirts, seductively tied silk scarves, and flirty berets (not to mention that chic bob!). She proved that you can be both feminine and strong. We should all take notes!

Mary-Kate and Ashley Olsen

Who would have thought those adorable twins on *Full House* would grow up to be two of the coolest fashion role models for our generation? MK and A are edgy; I'm not sure I would have the courage to wear what critics have dubbed their "bag lady chic." But these sisters flaunt their fearlessness. They launched two high-end fashion lines in 2008, Elizabeth and James, and the Row—and proved they have major designing chops as well as personal style. Brava times two!

Keira Knightley

I love the British aspect of her style, and how she mixes masculine and feminine. One day she does London street chic, and the next day she's superpolished at a premiere. She knows how to accentuate her figure and also how and when to take chances. Her style is always eclectic, but she *always* gets it right.

Rihanna

Coolness personified. She takes big fashion risks, mixing rocker with runway, but always with confidence. She puts out the vibe "I can be different and I'm okay with it." She doesn't just wear outfits, she rocks them!

THE BASICS: BUILDING YOUR STYLE

Every building needs a foundation, and the same goes for your style. The following are some basic pieces that can serve as building blocks for your wardrobe. The best part is, they all match with anything and everything—so you can create dozens of looks with just these ten easy pieces.

1 *Great-fitting jeans.*

I'm partial to Genetic Jeans and Current/Elliott at the moment and I went through a J Brand phase. But every girl has a brand that works best for her. I find that you'll get the most wear out of a darker wash; they're a little "dressier," so you can wear them to work as well as out at night. Do not feel like you have to spend a fortune for a fancy label. For how to find the perfect pair, see page 108. Another word of caution: although jeans with tears and holes are fine for weekends, you probably won't be wearing this look to the office. Keep them for when you can be casual or funk them up for a night on the town.

2 *A little black dress (or LBD).*

This piece is a simple, flattering dress in the most universally slenderizing color (although any dark color, like navy or chocolate brown, is also fine). But that's just the beginning. Add a leather jacket over it, and you've got an edgy outfit for partying; sweep on a cashmere cardigan and it goes to work. Dress it up, dress it down; the LBD is the most versatile piece of clothing you can own. I like my hemlines short; just above the knee is most versatile. But it's really up to you, as is the neckline and the length of the sleeves. Just make sure the cut flatters your figure, and that the material is fairly good quality so it will last and last and last (you don't want it to come apart at the seams after just a few wears). Since this is a staple, you can also spend a bit more for a good dress; you'll get a lot of wear out of it. But that said, you will often find a great LBD on the sale rack. If the price is right, snatch up a few in different cuts and weights. You won't regret it.

3 *Simple white, black, or heather gray tanks/tees.*

They work under anything—a suit jacket, a sheer blouse, a low-cut sweater—or tucked into a cute skirt. They should be soft, supple, and comfy. And when it's hot in the summer, you can wear them solo! If you find a bargain price, buy a bunch.

4 *A leather jacket.*

A motorcycle jacket is a cool classic; for elegance, you can't beat a luxe leather trench (my fave is by DVF!). Leather is expensive, but it's a long-term investment. The right leather jacket can go with everything from jeans to a sundress and last for years. Black is the most versatile color, though if you're bold, you can also get a lot of wear out of red, brown, a metallic hue, light gray, navy, or worn-out leather. Sometimes if I have a jacket that looks "too new," I'll put it on the floor and stomp on it!

5 *Cashmere knit scarves in any color.*

If my outfit needs a little "oomph," a bright scarf saves the day. Drape one around your neck; tuck it under the collar of a coat; sweep it around your shoulders as a shawl for evening; even tie it on your bag handle to add color. Wait till they go on sale after New Year's, then stock up on several shades. I have a nude one that I wear almost every day that matches everything. My mom always says if your neck is warm, you're set! Great as travel blankets as well.

6 *Black boots.*

I love them in all lengths: short, medium, tall, over the knee. You can really wear them with anything, from skinny jeans to a long, flowing skirt. But not all boots are created equal. The other day, Kelly cleaned out her closet and brought a bag of them to work. Roxy wanted this mid-calf-length studded pair with a squared-off toe. Hideous! I put the kibosh on it—and I know why Kel was trying to get rid of them!

7 *A black (or navy) blazer.*

Classic and classy. I toss one on with trousers, a floaty sundress, even a tee and jeans. I feel like it adds instant polish and "seriousness" to my outfit. Right now, I am into the oversize men's suit jacket look. It makes a simple outfit a little edgier.

8 *Simple heels (2–3 inches).*

Again, black is an easy choice since it goes with anything, but I am a huge fan of colorful shoes. Bright jewel tones jazz up a plain suit or a neutral-colored dress. The style, again, is up to you: pumps, mules, slingbacks, wedges, clogs, ankle straps . . . whatever you feel you'll get the most use out of for work/play. I stay away from anything too pointy—it reminds me of a witch.

9 *A sleek pencil skirt.*

The most versatile hemline hits just at the knee or slightly above/below, but show as much leg as you like. You can wear this day or night, paired with anything from a businessy blouse to a sexy tank. Pencil skirts are an ideal cut—sophisticated and versatile for day or night.

10 *An accessory that adds polish.*

My personal pick would be gold or silver hoop earrings, since they literally work with anything. But here's where your personality comes into play. You could choose a simple pair of studs (Claire's has tons that are cheap!), a dramatic pendant, layered long chains, a belt, a jeweled hair piece, or a stack of bangles. The goal is to find one "wow" addition that will work with a multitude of outfits. I often wear gold and silver chains wrapped around my wrist—another great use for a simple necklace.

WHAT I'M LOVING IN MY WARDROBE RIGHT NOW

Kate Spade cashmere sweaters
Isabel Marant jacket
Rachel Comey dresses and shorts
Whyred textured leggings from Opening Ceremony in black, navy, and maroon
Bandeaux bras
Fluffy soft socks, great for travel
DVF leather trench coat
DVF sequin jacket
Whitney Eve velvet dresses and slacks
Chanel nude purse
Topshop studded flats
Kain T-shirts
Marc Jacobs buckle boots
Lulu Frost, Fenton Fallon, Bing Bang, Made Her Think, and CC Skye jewelry
Giuseppe Zanotti shoes
Miu Miu shoes and bags
Converse leather high tops
Dr. Martens work boots
Chloe over-the-knee boots
Loeffler Randall boots (get the point? I love BOOTS!)
Victoria's Secret bathing suits
Valentino heels

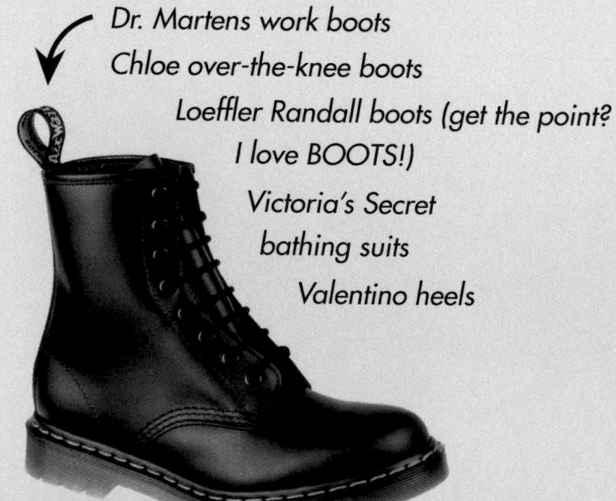

Topshop heels and bags . . . Topshop anything!
Gucci tapestry bag
Bloch flats; Sue London flats
Alexander Wang tees
Wolford tights
Current Elliot cords
Tacori stud earrings
White & Warren scarves and sweaters
Moschino jackets and shoes
Genetic jeans
Vena Cava jumper
Jen Kao dresses and skirts
Rebecca Taylor skirts and dresses
Be & D bags
Chanel chain messenger bag
Rebecca Minkoff studded bags
And duh! My own line, Whitney Eve! Especially my oversize blazer

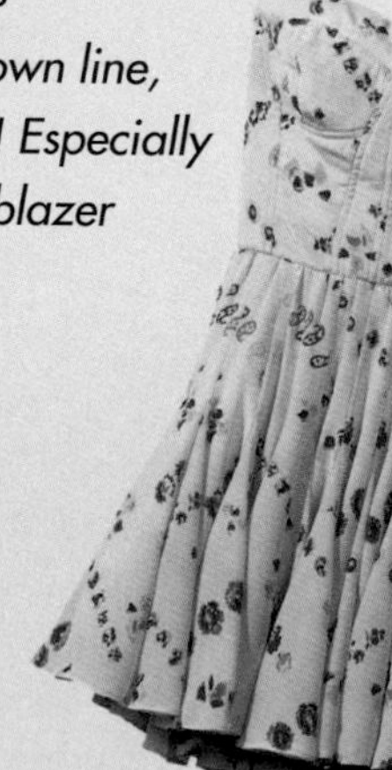

TRY IT . . . YOU MIGHT LIKE IT

Occasionally, you'll be surprised when you try something new on—something totally out of your fashion realm—and it looks *amazing*. I am lucky to have a truly gifted stylist, Lara Backmender, who pulls looks for events and the red carpet. She can spot an outfit on the rack or on the runway and know instinctively I'll flip over it. But every now and then, she'll throw me a curveball. She'll show me something and I'll think, "No, no, no . . . so *not* me." Then I remember, "Well, the woman is a professional . . . she is one of the best in the business!" And I almost always love it. What I'm saying here is this: have an open mind when it comes to fashion. If your best friend, boyfriend, sis, or even the salesperson suggests you try something on, don't automatically say no because it's something you wouldn't normally wear. It's hard to tell how something will look on you when it's on the hanger. But don't be peer pressured into wearing anything—the most important thing is that you feel comfortable in it. One of my pet peeves is when salespeople try to push things on me.

Sometimes you'll be shocked by what you end up being drawn to. Just ask my little sister, Paige, who recently "borrowed" a pair of boots from me that, in the past, she would not have been caught dead in. Paige went to school in the middle of Wisconsin and didn't need to be a fashionista. She looks at some of the things I wear in utter shock or horror. But then she moved back to L.A. and decided maybe it was time for a change. She called to inform me that she had found these crazy leopard platform ankle boots that I had left at home: "Whit, I tried them on and I am totally wearing them out this weekend!" I had to laugh just picturing my no-frills sis strutting out in those boots—but I'm so glad she's taking fashion risks and having fun!

The most important thing is that you feel comfortable in it.

SHOULD YOU BUY "HIGH"?

A lot of people are very label conscious. They think that paying a fortune for something designer equals status. Not me. I am a big believer in mixing high end and low end. I have no problem pairing an inexpensive T-shirt and jeans with designer heels. I love poking around through vintage stores and flea markets and scooping up steals. But I totally get it; sometimes, that pricey Chloe bag is just begging you, "Buy me!"

When you're just starting out, you probably don't have a lot of money to spend on high end. That's okay. Think about what you really want/need and what will be a good investment piece. For me, it's often a great bag. I carry one every day, so it's going to get plenty of airing. But it also has to be strong enough to tote all my stuff to and from work and survive getting knocked around on the NYC subways and streets. One of the first expensive bags I bought when I came here was a black Chanel backpack. I liked that I could have my hands free when I wore it, and also that I could wipe it clean if it got spilled on, dropped, trampled, and so on. So although it cost a lot more than the backpacks I used to carry in college, I have definitely gotten my money's worth out of it. I wear it every day—although my friends tease me that I've never outgrown my backpack days. Bags also *never* go out of style, unless it's one of those teddy bear backpacks my sisters and I wore in elementary school.

If you fall in love with an item that's not in your price range, don't give up so easily. Comparison shop at several stores. Ask the salesperson when it might be reduced—or if there are any coupons that will slice a percentage off the price tag. Google it and see if any of the discount fashion sites like bluefly.com, net-a-porter.com, ruelala.com, gilt.com, or shopbop.com carry it or a similar style. Even the department store Web sites have awesome sales. Often, you can find a bag you love in a "less popular" color—like green, pink, or purple. If you're like me and you love color, this is a good thing! Or sometimes "off-season" bags will be reduced, so you can get a great white

Gucci tote in the middle of the winter for a steal.

With a little ingenuity, you can find luxury for less. One of my friends was lusting over a sexy red suede Prada purse. On her editorial assistant salary, she just couldn't justify spending a week's salary when she had to eat and pay rent. Then she saw it one day for 40 percent off on bluefly! Score! Just make sure if you're buying designer off the Web, you're getting it from a trusted online merchant, like any of the ones mentioned. I had another, less-savvy friend who bought a YSL Muse bag off eBay, only to discover—after she paid $500 for it—that it was a fake.

You can also find a lot of clothing that has that couture "feel" without the hefty price tag. I love stores like H&M, Forever 21, Target, Urban Outfitters, Topshop.com, and pixiemarket.com. You can find everything from work clothes to evening wear for under $100! Another secret to looking like you spent $500 when you've really spent $50? Tailoring. A good tailor will be able to nip and tuck so that your clothes skim your body like they were custom-made. It generally will cost you an additional $20–$40 or so per item, but it's worth every penny if your outfit fits you like a glove.

SHOULD IT STAY OR SHOULD IT GO?

If you're going to buy new things, you have to purge your closets and drawers of items that no longer work for you. It kills me to get rid of my clothes. Seriously, I get totally sentimental over dresses I have worn to special occasions (even high school dances). I am emotionally attached! Sometimes I fear I'm becoming a hoarder! That said, I needed more space in my first place, and my wardrobe was taking up 99 percent of it. So I edited my closet—painful as it was. Buh-bye raggedy sweatshirts and sweats and bras that don't fit! Adios to ten of the same white tees and tanks! Get your best friend (someone who will be 100 percent honest with you) by your side for a give-away session. Should it stay or should it go?

Also, if you have sisters or female cousins, keep it in the family. That way you can always take it back if you regret giving it away.

Always swapping clothes with my sisters. In fact, that was the only thing we would ever bicker about.

Three simple rules will help you decide.

1 Don't hold on to ancient clothes thinking you'll lose weight. One pair of skinny jeans in the back of the closet is incentive enough.

2 When in doubt, try it on. If it doesn't fit, has frays, tears, or stains . . . it's outta there! Donate, donate, donate!

3 If you haven't worn something in the last year (or since high school!), you will probably *never* wear it again. Clear it out to make room for new stuff.

My closet before I got organized. I gave my sisters the pieces that just didn't inspire me anymore.

MY FAVE FASHION HITS AND MISSES

Sometimes you get it right . . . and sometimes you get it wrong. Really wrong. As in someone call the fashion police wrong. And you don't even realize it until you see a photo of yourself. Even someone who follows fashion (that would be me!) has the occasional "What was I thinking?" moment. Truth be told, we all have those days when our outfit is a little off or out of character—mine just tend to show up on TV or in the dos and don'ts pages of magazines.

Here are five of my chicest red carpet moments and four of my all-time worst fashion faux pas. All you can do is laugh at the bad ones (can you say "Ladybug dress"?) and learn from them. You can give away the don'ts to Goodwill or keep them as hand-me-downs—everything comes back into style eventually. I also find they sometimes make good Halloween costumes . . .

The Hits

I love these looks for lots of different reasons:

It always looks so fresh and effortless to pair your favorite jeans with a tank and feminine blazer. Wear them with a funky heel and there is really not much you have to do to look chic and cute without trying too hard. It's one of those outfits that you can throw on when nothing in your closet is working.

I wore this in Las Vegas on a trip when my suitcase got lost. I scoured the Caesars Palace Forum Shops and finally found this Marc Jacobs dress. It was so comfortable and had such a flattering cut. I'm a sucker for turtlenecks and anything short!

I was honored to be invited to the Council of Fashion Designers of America Awards representing Luca Luca in their gorgeous gown. The way the back crisscrossed was so sexy, and I just felt incredibly elegant. I loved the steel blue color as well.

This was a vintage beaded dress that my stylist, Lara, found. It had such gorgeous hand beading and the pastel color was so creamy and pretty. I faked a bob to show off the sheer top of the dress.

Another effortless look to try: tuck a white tank into a comfy, textured, high-waisted black skirt and you've got the cocktail/going-out-dancing look down! Those T-strap heels with the little black poof are still one of my favorites! I wore them to my first interview at DVF and got so many compliments.

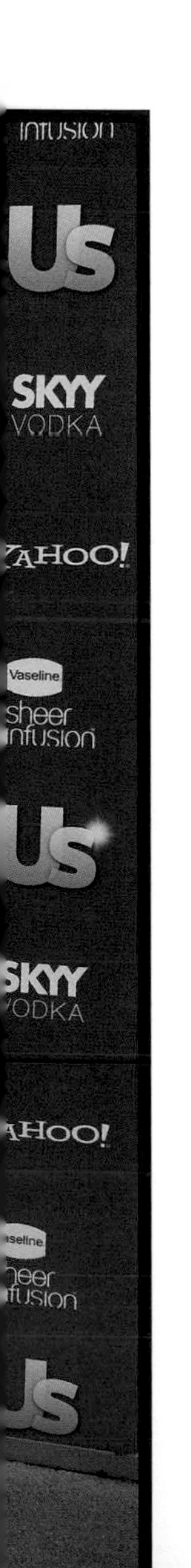

The Misses

Lucky me: if my parents didn't snap some of my worst outfits over the years, then the paparazzi sure did!

I actually loved the print on this dress, but the colors didn't quite suit me and the cut covered too much on top. It also doesn't look great in photographs!

This is another one of my favorite dresses, in theory, but I think the cutout in the middle was too ahead of its time.

The main problem with this look is that it's all around just too big. The hat is not a red carpet kind of accessory, the jacket is not a cute fit on me, and the jeans are way too big and long. I don't think I was planning on going out when I put this outfit on!

My ladybug look! Never dress like an insect unless it's Halloween. I have since banned ringlets from my hair "dos."

WHITTYISM: INSTANT SEX APPEAL!

Having a drab day? Put these on and you'll feel smokin' hot:

Lace panties.

No matter how hot your outfit is, there is no way in the world you're going to feel good about yourself if you're wearing "blah" undies. Splurge on a few fabulous pairs of lace ones. My faves are from Hanky Panky (hankypanky.com). They're so soft and comfy; they never ride up.

A sexy bra.

Cleavage can give you such a boost (pun intended), and if you don't have ample of your own, a great bra can work wonders. I'm personally bonkers over Bellabumbum bras, probably because they come in all these great, bright colors like peacock green and lilac (my fave). They're supercomfy; they never pinch, and you can literally lounge around your place in them. Just don't let the neighbors get an eyeful . . .

Stilettos.

Slip 'em on and you instantly feel sexy, skinny, and tall. Of course, if you're going to cram your feet into mile-high shoes, you better be prepared:

- Go shoe shopping in the afternoon when your feet are most swollen to get a real idea of what the heels will feel like after you've been in them for hours. Also, have the salesperson measure your foot—the way you used to when you were a kid—so you know the size is correct.
- If the shoe is really high and really pointy, try a half size to a full size larger than you'd normally wear. This will prevent pinching. And toe cleavage is not attractive!
- Buy some foot pads or insoles (I like the squishy gel ones)—they'll help prevent pain and blistering. I wore the ones by Dr. Scholl's to my sis's wedding and they saved the day!
- Break your heels in. You shouldn't buy a new pair and wear them out five minutes later for a night of dancing or a day at the office. Walk around the block in them or, at the very least, wear them around your home for a few hours, allowing the shoe to mold to the shape of your foot. Also, scuff the soles so you don't slip. You can also take a key and "engrave" some marks in the soles to make them less slippery.

ASK WHITNEY: WHAT SHOULD I WEAR WHEN . . .

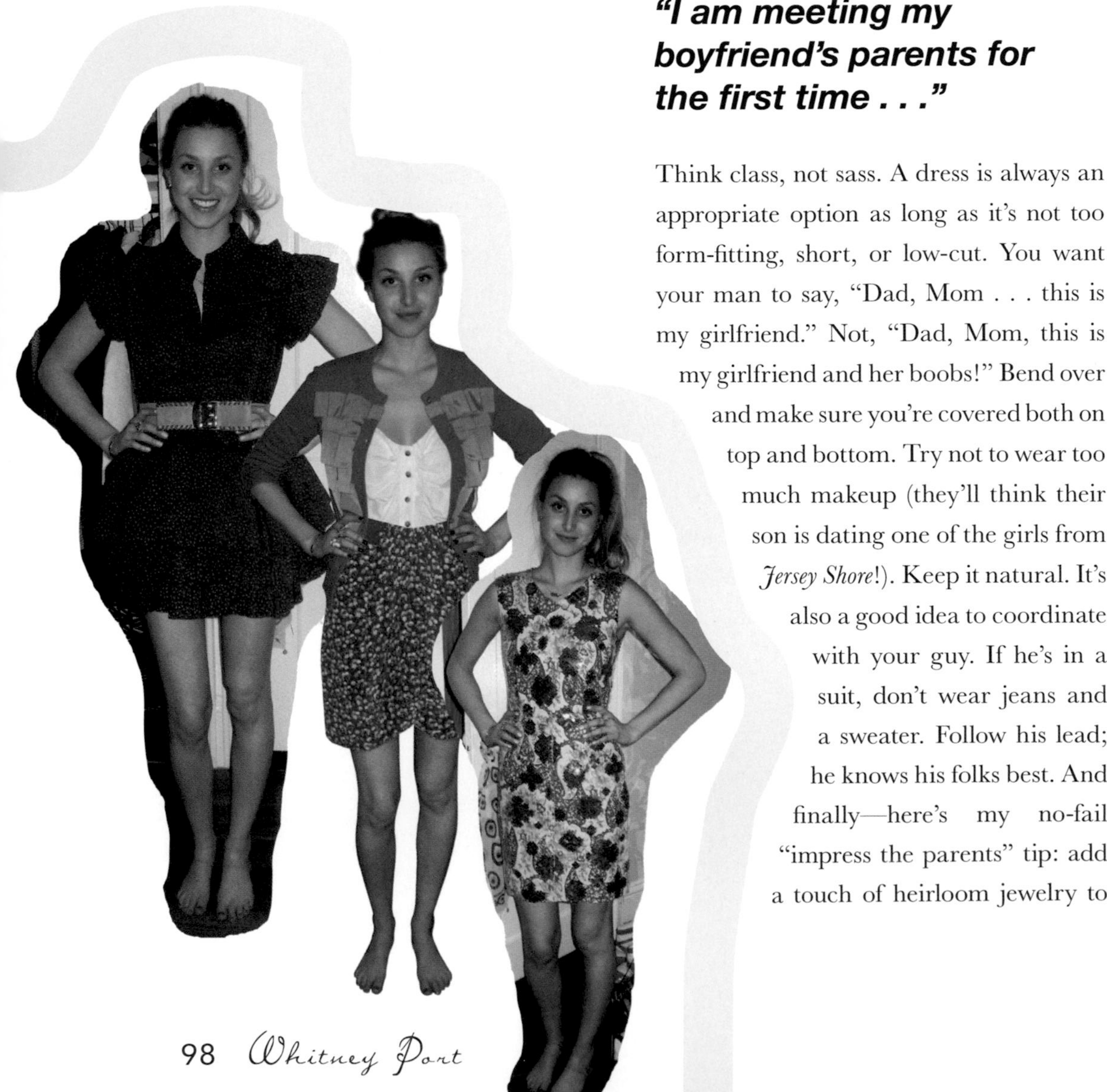

"I am meeting my boyfriend's parents for the first time . . ."

Think class, not sass. A dress is always an appropriate option as long as it's not too form-fitting, short, or low-cut. You want your man to say, "Dad, Mom . . . this is my girlfriend." Not, "Dad, Mom, this is my girlfriend and her boobs!" Bend over and make sure you're covered both on top and bottom. Try not to wear too much makeup (they'll think their son is dating one of the girls from *Jersey Shore*!). Keep it natural. It's also a good idea to coordinate with your guy. If he's in a suit, don't wear jeans and a sweater. Follow his lead; he knows his folks best. And finally—here's my no-fail "impress the parents" tip: add a touch of heirloom jewelry to your look, maybe a broach or a bracelet from your mom or grandmother. It will definitely be a conversation starter, and it shows you care about family (brownie points!).

"I have a blind date . . ."

It all depends on what you are doing and where you're going. In general, you want to avoid anything too revealing or over the top. Better to get to know him a little first before you bare your soul or any other private parts. For casual dates—like a movie—I would go for a skinny pant or jean, maybe a cute comfy sweater, and boots or flats. For something a little more formal—like dinner at a nice restaurant—you can't go wrong with a nice pencil skirt, sophisticated blouse, bomber jacket, and some comfortable heels. Most important, wear something that's "you," that makes you feel confident and at ease. I recently went on a dinner date and wore a deep purple velvet, long-sleeved V-neck Jill Stuart minidress with La Perla black tights and snakeskin heels. I added dangly chandelier earrings and wore deep red lipstick and did my hair retro chic wavy for drama. I felt alluring . . . but not overexposed.

"I am meeting my ex for drinks . . ."

Hot-hot-hot is the only way to go! Show him what he is missing! I met up with my ex Jay for drinks a few weeks after we broke up and I wanted to show him how together I was after we split. So I wore a slinky heather gray Jen Kao minidress—it had long sleeves but was skintight—with high heels and a little clutch, and I wore my hair down stick straight! You want your look to say, "You know you want me . . . and you blew it, dude."

"To the company holiday party . . ."

Remember who you're partying with: the people you work with. You don't want to be the water cooler conversation Monday morning. You should loosen up a little from your day look and dress festive—but keep cleavage in check. I'd suggest a V-neck sheath dress, a bright colored blouse and skirt, or a wide-leg pant with an embellished top. Dazzling accessories are totally acceptable: a great oversize or embellished clutch or chunky jewelry accents with fun hues.

"On a weekend getaway when I don't want to look like a slob . . ."

A few changes are all you really need. Stick to fabulous, versatile pieces that you can mix and match. My must-have for a short getaway is a maxidress. It works for most body types, packs easily, and can be worn with any type of sandals or flats for day and heels for evening. I take one in a soft, pretty pattern. I also never travel without a big, neutral-colored scarf. It can be used as a blanket while en route, a wrap to the beach or pool, or anytime you need a little extra warmth. Pack a comfy pair of shoes as well—a cute pair of comfy ballerina flats or a pair of Converse, Keds, or Vans work. And you can't go wrong with a comfy, baggy pair of jeans; a simple skirt with an elastic waist or a little ruffling; and a few cute tops.

"On a plane . . ."

Since it can get steamy standing in a crowded airport check-in line, and chilly on an air-conditioned plane, I always dress in layers that can be peeled off or added as needed. A sweater, hoodie, or thick scarf over a simple tank or tee will look stylish and also be practical. If only I always followed my own advice! I was recently on a red-eye from L.A., figuring I'd never see anyone I knew, and I wore sweats, UGGs, and an oversize long, hooded sweater. I looked a mess—and of course I bumped into two guys on the plane who were friends with the guy I'm dating. I only hope they weren't snapping pics and e-mailing them to him! Also, stick to comfy slip-on shoes—like ballet slippers or loafers. You'll be asked to take them off when going through security, and you might have to walk miles to the gate. Definitely not fun in heels! Don't forget to pack a pair of thick, fluffy socks in your carry-on—feet get so cold on planes.

On my way to Australia, all bundled up in my cashmere wrap.

My first view of Australia from the plane window.

Paige and I were folding clothes for a one-week trip. I always overpack; I like to be superprepared when I'm away. I also like to separate by categories: dresses, skirts, sweaters, shorts, etc., so when I unpack it's that much easier!

short numbers as well. Glamour isn't what it used to be. I love a dress that's simple and backless . . . I think it's so subtly sexy. You look good coming and going! The style and the glitz factor is up to you. Just make sure it flatters your figure and you can move in it. A friend of mine bought a gorgeous fish-tail gown for a formal benefit . . . only to discover she couldn't step up the stairs to the venue because it was so tight!

"The invitation says 'black tie' . . ."

Black tie means *very* formal. It doesn't mean you actually have to wear black; I certainly wear bold colors for evening affairs. But it does mean guests will be dressed to the nines, men in tuxes and women in long gowns of silk, satin, or sequins. You can be a little "looser" when you're younger—you can go shorter or show a little more skin. I brought my best friend, Andrea, to a black-tie event and we ended up agreeing that her short, beaded, one-shoulder silk dress was appropriate. Surprisingly, many other women were in

COLOR ME STYLISH!

Dearie, why so drab? If there is one fashion lesson you learn from me, let it be this: a little color is good for the soul! I believe in injecting a bit of brightness into every outfit. It brings out the highlights in your hair, warms your complexion, even adds sparkle to your eyes. Color makes you feel alive, energized, confident.

I believe in injecting a bit of brightness into every outfit.

Whether you add just a hint (a bright chunky chain necklace to a black dress) or pile it on (a bright scarf, boots, and bag with a tan trench), there are so many ways to weave it into your wardrobe. Don't be afraid to mix and match complementing colors. Some color combos I like are navy and light pink, lavender and nude, coral and turquoise. Certain hair colors/complexions look better in specific colors. It's hard to judge what your best palette is until you've tried on several colors. My best colors are definitely nude, lavender, coral, and aqua, while no can do yellow and orange.

Roxy, even though she claims to be the only California girl who wears black all the time, actually wore a Kelly green dress on a double date with me in the Meatpacking District—I think I'm beginning to rub off on her—and she absolutely glowed in the color. And my girlfriend Sammy rocked HOT bubblegum pink heels with a simple black dress to an art gallery opening. I love it! Both my girls admit that when you wear a little color, not only do you feel good . . . but you get a guy's attention. As Martha Stewart would say, "It's a good thing!"

Brunettes

Women with dark hair and dark eyes (including African Americans/Asians) look beautiful in bold, dramatic hues, like royal blue, crimson red, shocking pink, and emerald green.

Blondes

Women with lighter hair (or brunettes with light eyes) glow in springy shades, like lavender, mauve, nude, seafoam, and coral.

Redheads

Redheads look radiant in colors with golden undertones, like camel, beige, orange, gold, and chocolate.

Can you tell I love color and crazy patterns? Lime green, hot pink, bright yellow—bring it on!

BREAKING THE RULES

Never wear white after Labor Day. Don't combine gold and silver jewelry. Different patterns should never mix. It's time to ditch these tired rules! I see nothing wrong with wearing white year-round or donning glitter, shine, and embellishments during the day to spice up your daily grind. I think it's cool and fun to prove the rules wrong. I once wore a horizontal white-and-navy-striped Alexander Wang sweater with a Wayne plaid jacket. Not a natural combo, I know, but I thought it looked really funky together.

Just because you're not a size 0 and you have some curves doesn't mean you can't wear form-fitting clothes (can someone say J.Lo?). If you got it, flaunt it! And who ever said that you can't wear black with brown or navy was seriously mistaken. A black skirt and chocolate brown heels are a stunning mixture. And forget that old adage about your shoes having to match your bag. I recently spotted a woman on the street rocking a yellow oversize clutch with red pumps—what a look!

So what rules—if any—should you follow? This is the only one I subscribe to: don't wear something *just* because it's trendy. If you like it, fine. But if the only reason you're putting it on is because it's on some magazine's "In" list, I want you to think twice. It's like my mom used to say, "If someone told you to jump off a bridge with them, would you?" You need to develop your fashion backbone; resist the urge to splurge on stuff that isn't "you." Case in point: a few years ago, fedoras made a huge comeback. You know, the Dick Tracy–like detective hats? I passed. I don't care how many stars in Hollywood were wearing them. On me, they looked ridiculous.

I also believe you should never be *too* revealing with your outfits. Sexy is one thing; skanky is another. Adhere to the rules of common decency. Do not be caught with your pants down (or off!) in public or step out of a cab and flash the world your ass-ets. If your dress is low-cut, make sure there is something (such as double-sided Hollywood Fashion Tape) keeping your boobs under wraps. I know, sometimes it's an accident. But here's my golden rule: you can avoid major wardrobe malfunctions by simply checking every angle in the mirror as you sit, squat, bend, and jump. And don't forget to check yourself out in bright or natural light; how many times have I seen some poor girl strut into a party only to discover her dress or blouse was completely see-through? If you've done my check, you're good to go, lady.

JEAN-EOLOGY: FIND THE PERFECT PAIR

Studies say that women spend more time shopping for jeans than any other item of clothing, an average of three hours each shopping trip! But all that work can be worth it—jeans are easily the most versatile piece in your wardrobe. But with so many cuts, washes, and styles to choose from—not to mention an endless array of brands and price ranges—it truly is a mission to find one pair of denim that does it all. No matter what you think will look best on you—or even what has in the past—you have to try jeans on to really make certain. Choose a store that will let you take your time; go through fifty pairs if you feel like it. If they're snooty or trying to rush you to make a decision (or give up the dressing room), go somewhere else. I like to shop for jeans at department stores and Urban Outfitters. Skinny jeans are my fave because they elongate the legs, and I prefer them soft with some give, not stiff. An added bonus: if I can score a pair that also boosts my butt. My biggest thing with jeans is they have to be comfortable. I hate when they're too tight around my waist. My go-to style is low-waist, stretch, dark skinny jeans.

Your jeans should fit you *now;* not when you lose five pounds, not when you "break them in." Denim will stretch . . . but not that much. Figure 10 percent. If they're really tight in the waist or thighs, chances are they're not going to loosen up enough to really be comfy. So make sure can you sit, squat, and bend in them without cutting off circulation. And make sure your undies don't stick out when you bend over; that's just tacky.

Once you get your jeans home, always wash them in cold water. Warm water will shrink them. Turn them inside out to prevent fading, and skip the fabric softener (it can also break up the dye). Air-dry them instead of tossing them in the dryer, and dry-clean your dressier ones so they stay dark and crisp looking. Dirty side note: I may wear jeans five times or more before washing them. It's okay!

IT'S NOT WHAT YOU WEAR, BUT HOW YOU WEAR IT

Corny as it sounds, confidence is your best accessory. It doesn't matter how expensive or adorable that outfit is; if you feel awful about yourself, you'll look awful in it. I can look at a picture of myself and tell you if I was having a good day or a bad day by whether I have that frazzled look on my face. Which is a pity, because sometimes I really loved the outfit I was wearing and I let my bad attitude spoil the perfect photo op.

We all feel insecure about ourselves sometimes (I don't even want to tell you how nervous I was when they filmed me in a bikini on *The City*!). You think you'll grow out of it when you graduate from college. Adults don't doubt themselves, do they? Of course we do. We all have something we don't like about our bodies; some days, I am horrified by my love handles (now you understand the bikini anxiety). But no one is perfect. If you were, you'd be made out of plastic . . . or married to Seal. What I'm saying is, don't hate Heidi Klum because she's beautiful, and don't hate yourself because some days you feel anything but. Focus on your most fabulous features—your beautiful smile, your shiny hair, your sparkling eyes—not every flaw you can find in the mirror (and only if you look really, really hard). If you can't give yourself an attitude adjustment, call a friend or a family member for a pep talk before you set foot out that door. Stand up tall, hold your head high, take a deep breath, smile, and tell yourself, "I look *gooood*," and mean it. Suddenly, you'll radiate confidence and charisma; people will be drawn to you like a magnet and ask you what diet you're on or if you've cut your hair. Maybe they won't be able to put their finger on what it is that's different, but you'll know . . . you're "wearing" your confidence!

CHAPTER FOUR

PARTIES

o more keggers and Domino's pizza like in college. When you're in your twenties, soirees are about celebrating friendships, relaxing, and blowing off a little steam. I go to parties—mostly premieres or fashion events—at least twice a week. They're often glamorous and I get dressed up, but having people over in your personal space makes the event much more of a reflection of you. I always loved the idea of throwing a party in *my very own apartment.* It is a chance to showcase my lovely space, my unique taste, and celebrate the fact that (*Yes!*) I was not only surviving, but thriving in NYC! So with some help from my very talented party planner sister, Ashley, I have become quite the hostess over the last few years.

I was really excited about "entertaining"—it had such an elegant "adult" ring to it. I had been to an over-the-top dinner party on Olivia's posh Tribeca rooftop—that was quite the get-together. But I knew that *my* party would be different. It would be filled with cool people and great food, drinks, and music—and it would be intimate and relaxed, just like my apartment.

Roxy was my partner in crime—and truth be told, she talked me into it. I was living in my new apartment in the West

Ashley's wedding day: (left to right) Jade, Paige, Ryan, Ashley, Mom, Dad, and me!

Village—and she was staying with me at the time until she found her own place—so we decided to throw a housewarming party. I told Rox while we were planning it all out that we had to keep it low-key; the Board of my building didn't like music after eleven . . . but apparently that went in one ear and out the other. We agreed on a little cocktail party for a few friends. Instead, it was bigger than a block party—and the police wound up banging on our door! I was stuck at work at People's Revolution a little late that night, so Roxy had headed home to set up and greet our guests. By the time I got there, I saw the floods of people in my living room downing shots and drinking Roxy's signature superstrong jungle juice.

I'm not quite sure how it got so out of control (or who all those people were!). I freaked and just kept thinking, *Please, don't let me get kicked out of my new apartment!* Then came the sirens . . . Well, I did realize one thing: the next time I decided to throw a

Family portrait: (clockwise from back left) Ryan, Mom, Dad, Me, Ashley, Jade, Paige.

party in my place, I would (a) ask my sister Ashley for advice and (b) rein in Rox. That said, it wasn't all bad . . . just a bit chaotic.

So what makes a good party? Some people probably think an appearance by NYC's finest constitutes a pretty memorable bash (not me!). For others, it's all in the details. I have friends who go to great lengths folding little swan-shaped napkins and preparing exotic appetizers I can't pronounce, much less recognize. For other folks, it's about the ambiance: the right lighting, music, decorations. All of that helps, but if you ask me, the people are the most important component. If you have the people you love, your party will rock. There'll be intoxicating conversation, lots of laughs, even a few phone numbers exchanged. Pack a room with party poopers and your fete will fall flat. I always make

Singing karaoke with Roxy at my twenty-fifth birthday party in NYC.

sure I have a few chatty, colorful characters and some old reliable friends. You don't want everyone to necessarily know one another, but you do want people to feel comfortable. So make sure everyone you invite has at least has one "buddy" or acquaintance to schmooze with.

WHITNEY 101: HOW TO THROW A GREAT PARTY

Start with a fabulous idea.

By this, I mean figure out what the "theme" is. Are you throwing a Super Bowl Beer and Wings bash? An elegant sit-down dinner? A tea party for just the girls? Once you know the concept, you can plan the decorations, the guest list, and your menu—even if you only intend to order in.

Pick the perfect time.

A good party requires a good turnout. You may not want a huge party, but you still want people to come. Obviously, Friday or Saturday nights are the most popular times; you don't have to go to work the next morning. But sometimes a Sunday brunch can be just as fun! Just double-check that your party doesn't conflict with other popular events—like the World Series, Super Bowl, and so on—unless you are counting on that as part of your theme.

Invite your guests.

I know e-vites are all the rage because they're so easy (and free!), but I still think handwritten invitations are the way to go. They're so much more personal. Obviously if your party is last minute, you can call or e-mail. But it's a lot of fun to get creative. Your invite should obviously echo your theme. A friend of mine in New York threw a "Lobster Fest" on her rooftop and printed the who, what, where, and when in colored Sharpies on white disposable bibs. Very clever (and inexpensive!). When I was a kid, my mom always made our invitations by hand. It's so easy to hit a craft or paper store (like Michael's, Kate's Paperie, Staples) and score beautiful cardstock or paper you can print on or adorn by hand. Personalize your invite with stickers, scrapbooking cutouts, ribbons, glitter glue, photos, lace . . . whatever strikes your fancy. You can also find great templates online at sites like americangreetings.com. Make sure to include the essentials: date, place, time, theme (if any), BYOB, dating details (can you bring a plus one?) and include how to RSVP—via phone or e-mail. Maybe even come up with a cute poem for the invite. Ashley's husband is a songwriter and always comes up with the most witty invitation texts.

Decide what drinks and food to serve.

Make sure you have plenty for the number of people coming. I prefer to put things out buffet style and let people help themselves—it lets me mix and mingle and not worry about waiting on everyone. You should have enough chips, dips, nuts, and pretzels to keep people snacking all night. I would also suggest vegetable plates or different types of bruschetta for the more health conscious—I love to put out bowls of hummus and guacamole with crudités or cheese plates.

Size matters.

The number of people invited should be only ten greater than the space can hold (you hear that, Roxy?). Otherwise, you'll be packed in like a bunch of sardines. Not fun. A good rule of thumb: about 10 percent of your invitees will not attend. If you are inviting guests from out of town, the percentage is higher. If there are still people you've left off, create a "B" list. Just make sure your RSVP date leaves enough time till the party to invite your backups (at least a week is reasonable).

Set your sound track.

I like to put together a playlist of great tunes on my iPod—it can help to fill those awkward silences when the party is just starting. Some of my faves: Adele, the Kooks, the XX, La Roux, and Ratatat, and I love Dean Martin, Frank Sinatra, Etta James, John Legend, Tamarama, and Billie Holiday.

Drink up.

Unless you have a fully stocked bar and don't mind the expense, I would recommend having one type of drink to keep your costs lower—a signature cocktail, so to speak. Sangria is a great option, and you don't need to use a pricey bottle of cabernet. A simple red table wine for about $5 will do!

Make sure the space is set.

Do you have enough seats? Tables for people to put down plates/drinks? If not, borrow or rent. Make sure your guests have everything they'll need: enough napkins, plates, cups, and silverware—even TP in the bathroom! A good hostess covers all the bases. Don't forget the flowers!

HOW TO THROW A SMASHING . . .

Cocktail Party

Unless you have a lot of seating room (i.e., a dining table that has a leaf that folds out), a mix-and-mingle party—where you serve finger foods and cocktails—is the easiest to plan. Here's where you can get creative and devise a theme, like Mexican, Italian, Japanese. I love color themes, like a black-and-white theme à la Truman Capote, or even a metallic theme and playful themes, like "kid at heart" where you serve chicken nuggets, miniburgers, dogs, pizzas, and Popsicles! At one house party recently, the hostess devised her menu in her favorite colors, red and white. She put out tiny individual cups of pasta with a mushroom red sauce and platters of cherry tomatoes and mozzarella, and had pitchers of strawberry margaritas and white cosmos (made with white cranberry juice). Very cute! I also went to a really fun dessert party: little cupcakes, tarts, and cookies.

Be sure to scatter tons of napkins near the dishes—so people aren't dropping sauce or crumbs or wiping their fingers all over your furniture. If you have light-colored couches or chairs, buy inexpensive slipcovers or throws to protect them. They won't be as pretty, but you'll prevent stains, which are bound to happen with a big crowd!

Set the mood.

Dim the lights, fill the room with candles, and crank up some soft, subdued tunes (anything louder will be hard to talk over).

Serve up the apps.

I make sure to put out plates of different appetizers all around the room, so everyone can make their way around, chatting as they nibble and nosh. Cheese plates with grapes, Marcona almonds, and crackers and crudités with dip are a given, as are bowls of homemade bridge mix, pretzels, and chips. Beyond that, think savory snacks that are easy to pick up and pop in your mouth.

Mom's Chili Cheese Bites

Makes 32 "Bites"

My mama.

This is an easy hors d'oeuvre that takes ten minutes max to get in the oven (a big plus when you're rushing to get dressed). When we entertained at home, my mom would have to double the ingredients and whip up a larger 9 x 13 pan because I would gobble up at least half of it before guests would arrive!

4 tablespoons butter/margarine
5 eggs
¼ cup all-purpose flour
½ teaspoon baking powder
Dash of salt
1 (4 oz.) can chopped green chilies
½ pint small curd cottage cheese (1 cup)
2 cups shredded Monterey jack cheese

Preheat oven to 400 degrees Fahrenheit (205°C). Melt butter/margarine in a 9-inch-square pan in the oven (tip pan to coat bottom and sides). In a large bowl, beat the eggs, then stir in the flour, baking powder, and salt. Add the melted butter/margarine to the preceding; set pan aside. Stir in the chilies, cottage cheese, and jack cheese; mix until blended. Pour batter into the butter/margarine-coated pan. Bake 15 minutes. Reduce heat to 350 degrees and bake 30–35 minutes longer or until lightly browned. Cool slightly and cut into small squares. May be frozen. If frozen, before serving reheat in a 400-degree Fahrenheit oven for 10 minutes or until hot.

Easy Hummus Recipe

Makes 1 Cup

A Whitney staple. Hummus is one of my fave foods, and it's even better when you make it from scratch (you can really taste that garlic!). Feel free to go crazy and serve it with any kind of vegetables, pita, or chips.

½ cup chopped parsley
1 big garlic cloves minced
½ teaspoon salt
3 tablespoons tahini sesame seed paste (can be purchased at most grocery stores or a gourmet shop)
4 tablespoons lemon juice
1 (15½ oz.) can garbanzo beans, drained

Place all ingredients in a blender or food processor fitted with a metal blade. Process until smooth. Refrigerate several hours before serving, may be stored in fridge up to one month. Serve cold as a dip or spread.

Sangria in a Snap

2 bottles of red wine, standard size
2 oranges, cut into bite-size pieces with the skin on
2 apples, cut into bite-size pieces with the skin on
1 handful of any type of berries
12 oz. of 7-Up
1 half bottle Prosecco

This can be made ahead of time and stored in the refrigerator. Add the 7-Up and Prosecco at the end, right before you serve, to make sure the fizz holds. Make sure to tell guests to eat the fruit, too—it's the best part of sangria!

Toaster Oven Apps Party

My family will tell you that I am not exactly an Iron Chef in the kitchen. My mom, my sister Ashley, and my sis Paige—they can make a feast out of anything in the fridge. I am not as talented in the kitchen. In fact, when Roxy and I first decided to throw our apartment party, I was shocked to discover I was missing one very important thing I needed: an oven. I called my mom and told her my dilemma. "Whitney," she said with a sigh, "how could you not know you didn't have an oven?" Probably because I never use one! I cook in my toaster oven because it's smaller and easier for just one person. Well, she came up with a great menu for the party that I could do, just using my trusty toaster oven. It can be done, I swear!

Serves 6–8

1 sourdough baguette (or favorite)
3 red tomatoes finely chopped
Olive oil
Salt and pepper
Parsley or oregano (optional)

Cut half-inch slices of the baguette on the bias. Finely chop all the tomatoes and place in a mixing bowl. Add salt and pepper to taste as well as the parsley/oregano. Mix it all together with olive oil. Brush the sliced bread with olive oil. Put in the toaster oven until crispy. Remove and, while warm, put the marinated tomatoes on top. Ready to serve!

Goat Cheese Phyllo Pouches

Serves 8–10

1 package of phyllo dough
1 log of goat cheese
Olive oil

Defrost the phyllo dough. Take 2–3 pieces and brush the top piece with olive oil. Place one small dollop of goat cheese on dough and fold to look like ravioli. Place pieces in the toaster oven and cook until they are warmed through the center (approx. 12 minutes).

Mini Individual Pizzas

Fresh pizza dough (or frozen)
Tomato sauce (you can use your favorite store-bought one such as Giorgio Baldi, but I prefer homemade or just "white")
Shredded mozzarella cheese
Any other toppings you like (e.g., pepperoni slices, peppers, onions, olives)

Go to your local pizza place and buy some freshly made dough. You can also use frozen dough (leave time to defrost) or Boboli. Flatten out your dough, till it's approximately the size of a CD. Make sure to leave a border (about an inch all the way around) for your crust. Pour some marinara sauce on the dough and spread. Top with the mozzarella cheese and any toppings you desire. Toast for 15–20 minutes until dough is cooked and cheese is melted. Serve immediately!

Sit-Down Dinner

I am all about ease, but I believe that a sit-down dinner calls for a little "formality." Don't just put out paper plates and cups; break out the china, even if you don't have a full matching set. Just like I love to mix and match patterns and colors in clothing, I do the same thing with my plates, saucers, and serving dishes. There's nothing wrong with having every setting look different. I've inherited a few pieces from my mom and grandma; others I've picked up for really cheap at flea markets or on sale at places like Z Gallerie, Urban Outfitters, Anthropologie, and Target. You can mix delicate florals with elegant stripes—then put a solid bright bowl or appetizer plate on top. Have fun with it! Same goes for your linens and napkins. All different patterns of florals are cute, too.

Set the mood.

I love fresh flowers on the table—it just lends an air of elegance. For the amateur arranger, it's important not to pick more than three types of flowers, and stick to a low vase—so guests can see each other eye to eye across the table. I love flowers that really scent the room, like sweet peas, gardenias, lilacs, and roses. My grandmother always had the most amazing sweet peas growing near her front door, and my mom has a gardenia bush in our backyard. Every time I smell these flowers, I smile. If you don't have a backyard to pick from, simply hit the local florist. Ask what flowers are in season; they'll be the least expensive. In general, carnations, daisies, and camellias are cost-friendly; peonies, tulips, and orchids will run you the most. Also, white flowers tend to be more expensive since they bruise easily.

I love flowers that really scent the room, like sweet peas, gardenias, lilacs, and roses.

Serve up.

A classic meat or chicken dish—or for a healthy crowd, something veggie. Serve something that will look elegant and gourmet without being too difficult. The last thing you want is to look stressed from an Iron Chef–difficult recipe when your guests arrive!

Balsamic Marinated Skirt Steak

Serves 3–4

½ cup balsamic vinegar
¼ cup olive oil
3 rosemary sprigs
3 gloves garlic, thinly sliced
1½ pounds skirt steak
Kosher salt and freshly ground pepper

Combine balsamic vinegar, olive oil, rosemary, and garlic in a glass or plastic dish, and stir. Add skirt steak and coat well with the marinade. Cover and refrigerate for at least 30 minutes, and up to 2 hours. Preheat broiler or grill. Remove steak from marinade, and transfer to a rimmed baking dish. Season meat generously with kosher salt and pepper on both sides. Place under broiler or on grill and cook about 3 minutes. Turn over, and cook for 3 minutes more for medium rare. Transfer to a cutting board to rest for 5 to 10 minutes. Slice thinly across the grain, and serve.

Great-Grandma Eva's Baked Vegetables

Serves 6

I love this over brown rice; it's a great vegetarian dish, and I take the leftovers to work for lunch. I even eat it cold!

8 carrots, peeled and cut with a french fry cutter
8 stalks of celery, cut
1 large yellow onion
1 green pepper
1 or 2 large tomatoes
2 tablespoons butter or margarine
1 cup uncooked white or brown rice
1 large bottle of tomato juice
Mushrooms (optional)
Parmesan cheese

Preheat oven to 325 degrees Fahrenheit. Wash and cut all vegetables into large bite-size pieces. Place all ingredients in a mixing bowl and stir; add salt and pepper to taste. Spray a large casserole with nonstick cooking spray and transfer all ingredients. Cook covered for 30 minutes. Stir well and re-cover, then cook for another 45 minutes or until vegetables are tender. Serve immediately with grated Parmesan cheese.

Paige's Lemon Chicken

Serves 6–8

This is my sis's simple recipe. It tastes amazing served on a bed of fresh arugula with some shaved Parmesan cheese. I also love that it cooks on a stovetop (a good thing for me, since when I first made it, I didn't have a working oven!).

Olive oil
8 chicken breasts
2 lemons
1 tablespoon minced garlic
½ cup kalamata olives
¼ cup kalamata juice
½ cup white wine
Salt and pepper

Place the chicken in a large Ziploc bag and pour the juice of one lemon and the minced garlic into the bag, along with the olives and olive juice. Add the white wine, then salt and pepper to taste. Let this marinate in the fridge. After a few hours, take out of fridge and allow to reach room temperature (approx. 30 minutes). Pour all contents from the bag into a roaster. Cook on both sides until golden brown. After the chicken is browned, you can put one lemon slice on top of each breast, then cover and cook for another 20 minutes.

Blowing out the candles and making a wish!

Please Celebrate with

Whitney

as she turns 25!!

Friday, March 12
8:00 pm

Cecconi's
8764 Melrose Avenue
West Hollywood

RSVP to Ash
310.709 6

The invitation for the party was white text letter-pressed into tulip-colored paper and mounted.

CECCONI'S

Whitney's Birthday Dinner
March 12th, 2010

Starter
Ahi tuna tartare, chili & mint

Mid course
Chopped vegetable salad

Entrees
to choose

Baked gnocchi 'Romana', gorgonzola

Roast branzino filet, cherry tomatoes & black olives

Grilled chicken, vegetables

Dessert
Cake

A printed menu was placed at every guest's seat underneath their napkins.

My sister Ashley custom designed this stamp to tie in to the overall look.

WHITNEY'S TWENTY-FIFTH BIRTHDAY

My twenty-fifth birthday party was held at Cecconi's in West Hollywood last year on Friday, March 12th. The event was designed and planned by BK Events (which is my sis Ashley's company). It wasn't an official surprise, because I knew it was happening, but all Ash told me to do was choose the color palette and show up. The rest she kept under wraps. I wore a white Cinderella-esque Manoush dress with Giuseppe Zanotti heels and Bing Band earrings.

I was one of the first to arrive. It was a very surreal moment, but I embraced it. I felt very lucky to be surrounded by so much love. There is not much more you can ask for at any age. Twenty-five is a big number and comes with a lot of expectations, but if you have support, compassion, and loyalty, everything else is a cakewalk.

My family, Mom, Dad, Ryan, Ashley, Evan, Paige, and my cousin Jackie—everyone except Jade, who was stuck in Wisconsin at college—was there, as well as my best friends from long, long ago and a couple of new ones. I was so happy that everyone from all walks of my life could spend time together and get to know one another.

The party's design was a modern interpretation of a tea party. The floral arrangements, designed by BK Events and Sticks & Stones, were pink peonies that filled teapots and cups and saucers. The room was candlelit and had a very whimsical feel, complete with accents of pink tulle. Guests sat at two long, supper-style tables.

The menu featured all my faves. As guests arrived there was a small cocktail reception on the outdoor veranda. Guests were served rosé champagne and mini pizzettas on gold-and-white monogrammed cocktail napkins. Inside, the restaurant served ahi tuna tartar followed by a chopped fall vegetable salad. For the entrée, guests had a choice of potato gnocchi, grilled chicken, or branzino. And for dessert (my fave part of the meal!), Ash ordered my favorite birthday cake, that I have every year: the mixed berry cake from Sweet Lady Jane Bakery in L.A.

I'm on my way to the party! I wore a white Manoush dress. The top was fitted and the skirt was a "poof," which kind of matched my favor table.

My first look at the decorated room on the night of the party.

The party favor table linen was made out of white tulle and looked like a huge ballerina tutu! Favors were wrapped in pink tissue and pink tulle, and tied with gold foil ribbon. A glittering gold peacock feather was added as an accent.

Guests were seated at two long tables in a private room at a restaurant in West Hollywood. The room is called the Butterfly Room because of the amazing heart and butterfly art hanging in the back.

Each place setting had a hand-calligraphied name card, gold-sequined napkin bands (hand sewn by my sis Ashley), and an Esperance rose to top it off.

Turquoise chairs, which are part of the restaurant's design, offset the pink-and-gold theme of my birthday bash. It added a nice pop of color to the candlelit room.

The glitter candles were custom ordered and dipped in four tones that flowed with the décor: champagne, almond, gold, and blush.

The linens for the party were gold silk underlays with fourteen-karat-gold silk thread embroidery on ivory French lace.

This layout was kind of tricky when it came to seating assignments. Since the room could only hold thirty, there were no bad seats, but separating sixteen and fourteen guests can be hard.

e and Joanna during the outdoor cocktail portion of the party.

Me with Sophia.

Me and Andrea during dinner.

Packing up at the end of the night.

Brunch

After a tough workweek, there's nothing nicer than getting together with friends on a Saturday or Sunday morning. Call the party for a reasonable hour (around noon) so everyone can sleep in.

Set the mood.

Channel your inner Martha Stewart and make your brunch bright and cheery: whether you serve sit-down or buffet style, everything on the tables should be colorful and feel like a breath of fresh air. Brunches can be casual or fancy, your choice. I prefer to keep it all very low-key (who wants to fuss on a weekend?). I use mismatched glasses in rainbow colors and drape the tables in swags of different fabrics. I even place little decorative pillows on the chairs so people can relax.

Serve up.

Breakfast classics . . . yummy comfort foods that remind everyone of home. You can sprinkle in chocolate chips or fresh fruit in pancakes and top with whipped cream or powdered sugar. But I like my pancakes and waffles "straight up" with warm syrup. Make it easy on yourself if you have a big crowd coming: blend all the dry ingredients and keep in the pantry in Tupperware or a Ziploc bag. All you have to do is add the wet ingredients in the morning and you're ready to start flipping . . .

Tara's Pancakes

Makes 4–6 Pancakes, Depending on Size

Tara is my mom's best friend and she gave Mom this great recipe. I beg my mom to make these for me whenever I come back home!

1 ¾ cup flour
1 teaspoon salt
1 ¾ teaspoons baking powder
3 teaspoons sugar
1 to 1 ¼ cups milk

2 eggs
6 tablespoons of butter (melted)

In a large bowl, sift together the flour, baking powder, salt, and sugar. Pour in the milk, eggs, and melted butter; mix until smooth. Heat a lightly oiled griddle or frying pan over medium-high heat. Pour or scoop the batter onto the griddle, using approximately ¼ cup for each pancake. Brown on both sides and serve hot.

Belgian Waffles

Makes 8 Small Squares or 2 Large Belgian Waffles

My mom is a master at making these. I always liked them filled with chocolate chips!

1 ¾ cup flour
1 tablespoon sugar
1 egg
1 ½ cup beer (not light)
¼ cup oil
1 teaspoon vanilla

Mix all ingredients and allow to stand for two hours or more at room temp. Grease waffle iron before using.

Frozen Bellini

½ cup peach nectar or purée
¼ cup peach schnapps
Crushed ice
¾ cup chilled champagne or Prosecco

Mix all ingredients in a blender until smooth. Pour into champagne flutes and garnish with a peach. Cheers!

A Dessert Party

This is a fun twist on a potluck dinner: you make the main meal, and ask guests to BYOD (bring your own dessert)—enough for everyone. Sweet! Of course, you'll want to make a few of your own treats to set the bar high . . . I love the idea of creating a sundae buffet with all the fixin's (M&Ms, gummy bears, crushed graham crackers, crushed Oreos, chocolate chips, sprinkles, chopped nuts, shredded coconut, etc.) or minitarts (just buy some mini premade pie crusts, top with chunks of apple, pear, or peaches, and bake) à la mode.

The right light.

Everything looks better in dim lighting. A really cheap way to make your space more inviting is by installing a dimmer on your regular lighting switch. You don't even have to be an electrician to be able to do this; all you need is a screwdriver. Or, of course, if you're using all lamps like I used to, get some lower-watt bulbs, or try a sheer piece of fabric over a few of the shades to set the mood. Turn the lights down low and light some candles when it's time for the final course of the meal.

Lay it all out.

After the dinner, prepare a pretty, large, buffet-style table to display everyone's goodies. Make sure you have plenty of small plates (glass or see-through plastic ones are great; they won't distract from the decadent desserts!) and serving forks/spoons. I like to go around the room and ask who brought what and what the story is behind each dessert.

Makes 2 Cups

This is my mom's decadent creation! I pour it on top of coffee ice cream. Yum! It's ultraimpressive; it actually hardens as it cools. I keep the leftovers in a Tupperware container in the fridge, then pop it into the microwave and use it for dipping fruit.

½ pound butter or margarine (2 sticks)
1 (12 oz.) package semisweet Nestlé chocolate chips
1 cup coarsely chopped walnuts or pecans (optional)

In a double boiler over hot (not boiling) water, melt butter or margarine and chocolate chips, stirring until smooth. Stir in nuts. Serve hot. May be refrigerated and reheated.

Makes 2 Dozen Cookies

A classic Jewish pastry! It's served on the holiday of Purim—which is kind of like Halloween, because you get to dress up in costumes but it's in the winter. I actually love hamantaschen for breakfast with coffee, so I make it any time of year. Purim celebrates the Jews' freedom from Haman—an evil guy with a signature accessory: his large, triangular-shaped hat. So that's why the pastry is a triangular shape, the shape of Haman's hat. I just love food that incorporates fashion!

2 cups flour
½ pound butter
2 (8 oz.) packages cream cheese

1 jar jam/jelly (my mom uses the traditional apricot or raspberry, but you can use your favorite)
1 egg (yolk only)
Chopped nuts (optional)

Combine the first three ingredients and refrigerate (overnight recommended). Roll dough to nice workable thickness, about ¼ inch thick. Cut circles 3 inches in diameter. Put ¼ teaspoon of your favorite jam or jelly in center of each circle. You may add nuts. Moisten edges with egg yolk. Pinch corners to form a triangle. Bake at 375 degrees for 10 minutes.

Wendy's Fudge

My aunt Wendy taught me how to make this, and trust me, there is never enough. If you get invited somewhere at the last minute, don't panic, this is a great hostess gift!

4 cups chocolate chips
4 cups mini marshmallows
1 cup peanut butter (crunchy)

Melt chocolate bits in a microwave or a double boiler for 1 minute. Stir and repeat at 20-second intervals until melted. Spray a rubber spatula with a nonstick cooking spray and stir in peanut butter. Fold in marshmallows and stir until covered with chocolate. Pour into a 9-by-13-inch foil-lined pan. Chill in refrigerator for at least 15–20 minutes until hardened. Lift out foil and cut with a pizza wheel into bite-size pieces.

Drink up.

A sweet signature cocktail for the evening! To garnish, dip the rim of the glass in cocoa powder or drop an unwrapped Hershey's Kiss into the drink.

Vodka Espresso

This can be served instead of coffee!

1oz. vodka
½ oz. Godiva mocha liqueur
1 oz. cold espresso
1 splash simple syrup

At Coachella with one of my BFFs Sydney.

In Australia on a night out with Paigey.

On a boat taking a sunset cruise around Sydney Harbor with new friends met in Australia.

GUESTS GONE WILD

Practically every bash I have thrown or attended had a few of these types. Recently, a girl at one of my parties got really drunk and hit on Roxy's boyfriend (I could see the steam coming out of Rox's ears). Here's how to handle unruly guests.

The lush.

She's been doing shots of Jägermeister all night and has now fallen facedown in your fondue pot. She's drunk as a skunk and still begging for more booze.

What to do: Offer to call her a cab and get her home before she hurls; if she drove, make sure you take her car keys.

The slut.

In just a few hours, she's made out with your coworker and your brother, and now she's organizing a game of strip poker.

What to do: Kindly tell her to keep her clothes on. But unless she's offended anyone (chances are none of the guys will be complaining), there's little you can do about her "friendliness." If she's really annoying you, ask her to leave. She'll probably be happy to take one of her boy toys home for the night.

The loudmouth.

His comments are rude, lewd, and giving you a throbbing headache. This blowhard can't keep his opinions to himself or his voice down to a dull roar.

What to do: Be as direct as he is: explain that you have neighbors and he has to take it down a notch or leave the premises. If he doesn't get the message . . . try using a whistle.

The leech.

She's glued to your side, barely letting you spend a minute with any of your other guests.

What to do: This clinging vine is probably just feeling insecure. Does she know anyone else at the party? Is she shy? Make introductions and try to find her someone she has something in common with to talk to. If all else fails, ask a kind friend to "babysit" her for a few minutes so you can get a break.

LAST-MINUTE PARTIES

It was a weekend and I was bored . . . so on a totally Whitney whim, I decided, "Let's have a party!" I called a few friends who were free and they said they'd be over in a few hours. Which left me wondering . . . "WHAT HAVE I DONE?" After I calmed down, I realized this wasn't a reason to stress. This is one of the best parts of living on your own; you don't have to ask anyone's permission to throw a party. You just do it! With a little ingenuity—and a few takeout menus—I knew I could pull it off.

I do have to warn you, though, to keep a last-minute party small and manageable; that means five to ten guests, not fifty. Not only do you have to coordinate your entire event, but you have to figure out what you are going to wear, do your hair, and so on. The first thing to do is make a list—that way you can see what you are up against. Also, don't be proud and think you have to cook everything yourself. Order in. I even found a place right in SoHo that delivers gourmet bite-size cupcakes for dessert (bakedbymelissa.com). There's also nothing wrong with phoning your local supermarket, deli, Chinese takeout, or pizza place and asking them to put together a few platters. Break out the china; it makes even a slice of pepperoni look pretty. Have everyone bring a bottle of wine, and you're all set. Instant soiree!

This is one of the best parts of living on your own; you don't have to ask anyone's permission to throw a party. You just do it!

Because my sis has her own party-planning biz (BK Events, bkevents.net), she's the perfect person to answer all my questions about cooking, serving, and hostessing.

Whitney: Should you tell people where to sit at the dinner table?

Ashley: This all depends on how many guests you are entertaining. If you have a lot of bodies—and a few tables—placecards can help prevent people from getting "stuck" next to someone they don't know/like. On the flip side, you can also "place" people together—which is great if you're trying to fix up two friends! But if it's a really casual dinner with only a few folks, there's really no need for that. Let everyone take a seat where they're comfortable. There are many nontraditional ways to make seating cards, too. You don't have to be superformal. You can write names on something cute—like a napkin ring or even in icing on a piece of chocolate!

Whitney: What if you make a dish . . . and someone tells you they don't eat what you're serving? Should I ask people what they will/won't eat?

Ashley: If you are entertaining at home, you should always have a vegetarian option as part of the menu. This way, if guests don't like the main dish, they don't go hungry! A simple soup or a salad is great; or some roasted veggies/potatoes to accompany the entree. Otherwise, you don't need to "clear" the menu beforehand—unless you have a guest of honor, and you want to celebrate him/her by making a favorite dish.

Whitney: What do you do if you burn dinner right before the party?

Ashley: Obviously, it's important to make a timeline for cooking. That way if you make mistakes, you can always redo a dish. But if the situation does arise—and your guests are at the door—call for delivery! Your guests will understand and it makes for a good laugh later.

Whitney: Do I have to serve red wine with meat? Can I serve it with chicken or fish?

Ashley: For years people have believed you needed to serve white with chicken and fish, and red with steak. You don't have to stick to those *exact* rules, but it's important to keep a balance between food and wine. You want to make sure one doesn't overpower the other. If you are serving a heavy dish, you would need a richer or stronger wine to complement it. Likewise, a lighter entree would need a softer wine. I suggest a red with beef or lamb, but if you want to switch it up and serve a red with fish or chicken, go with a pinot noir. It's a lighter red.

WHITTYISM: WHEN YOU'RE THE GUEST

You don't want to show up empty-handed. Most people bring the party host/hostess a bottle of wine, a box of chocolates . . . *boring*. I like to give something a bit more out of the box! If the host is an old friend, how about a scrapbook or wine-of-the-month club membership. It's also fun to bring a board game for all to play, like Taboo or Scattergories. Bake something: I often bring someone their fave dessert—my best friend, Joanna, loves this chocolate chip banana bread that my mom bakes so I wrap up a loaf for her. I think playlists are also great gifts. I like to make a CD and bring it to pop on at the party. Or—if unusual is what you're after—how about some whimsical trash bags? Findgift.com has some wacky ones printed with goldfish; tell your host they come with an offer to help her clean up after the gang has cleared out.

CHAPTER FIVE

DATING

Everyone always says—my mom included—you have to kiss a lot of frogs before you find your prince. She wasn't kidding; I have locked lips with loads of toads. But that's okay, because dating—really putting yourself out there and being open to new people, new relationships—is the only way to figure out what and who you want.

Dating in your twenties is very different from dating in your college years. When you're an adult, it feels like suddenly everyone is looking for a "serious" relationship. There's pressure to settle down, to couple off, to not be "the last one" of your girlfriends to get engaged. But sometimes it's hard to distinguish Mr. Right from Mr. "Great Body, Well-Dressed, but Forgets to Call on Saturday." Although I don't believe you have to lasso the first guy who seems like "marriage material," I do think you have to consider the kind of person you want to be with for the long run. Don't necessarily rule out all the others (they can be fun, even if they're not your perfect match, and teach you what you do and don't want or what you can or cannot handle), but at least start to think about yourself—your needs, your desires, your goals—and how someone else might fit into that picture.

Dating on a reality TV show is even *more* complicated. Most people have to deal with their pals fixing them up—I also have to deal with my producers playing matchmaker! On a recent photo shoot, one of them asked me to "check out" the photographer (who was apparently checking me out the entire time). He was French; he was artsy; he drove a motorcycle—they thought he'd be a good guy for me. Truthfully, I didn't feel any electricity between us on the shoot, but I said, "Sure . . . why not?" I always trust my first impression. Rarely am I surprised, but it's worth giving guys a chance. I think it's fine to meet a guy for drinks or a coffee—even if you don't think it's going to amount to much. It's a few hours out of your life; if you're truly not into it, then keep it quick. That takes a lot of the pressure off.

Accept the invitations, take chances, and enjoy yourself!

Like almost everything in life, relationships are all about trial and error. My old roommate Erin used to tell me to play the field; that's what dating is about. She'd say, "You go out, you see a couple of people, then you see some people less and less . . . until you wind up exclusive, if that's what you want." I wish it were that easy!

Love can happen when you least expect it, as long as you're open to the experience. So accept the invitations, take chances, and enjoy yourself! It can be a lot of fun if you're willing to go on a few fix-ups or have some flings, with the only expectation that this is going to be *interesting.*

I grew up reading fairy tales, where shining knights on white horses ride in and sweep princesses off their feet. I don't know if I believe those stories (Prince Charming better hurry up—my feet are killing me!), but I do believe in love. I believe that two people can share an incredible, deep, once-in-this-lifetime connection and commitment to each other. I believe love isn't just about lust (though that part is certainly fun); it's about caring deeply about someone. I also think friendship has to play a big part. Your partner, your husband, your significant other—whomever he/she is should also be your best friend, your confidant, your support system. That person should love you for you, for every little quirk and craziness that drives other people up a wall. When you find that someone . . . you know. My wise married sis, Ashley, always tells me you should never settle, and be totally prepared to be vulnerable.

That said, I also don't feel you need a man in your life to make you complete. There's nothing wrong with being single! My family raised me to be an independent woman (although when I go home my sisters are always looking after me). I know there are plenty of ladies out there who feel totally lost without a love in their life. I don't feel this way at all. I'm okay being single in the city. And trust me, that's much more attractive to a guy than a girl who reeks of desperation. It is also so much more empowering to be alone than to stay in a dysfunctional relationship purely because it's comfortable.

My fifth-grade crush, Michael Tayafelt.

My first official high school boyfriend, Sean.

My current boyfriend, Ben.

I have been in four major relationships in my life: a high school boyfriend who I was on and off with for a couple years; a college boyfriend who was my first "true love"; my first romance in NYC (a certain Australian rocker!), which quickly turned into a relationship; and a more mature relationship filled with compassion and vulnerability. I would love to take certain qualities from all my boyfriends and mesh them together to make the perfect man. But I know "perfect" is only a figment of one's imagination. Still, if I could take my first boyfriend's empathy and ability to listen, pair it with my second boyfriend's humor and charm, mix it up with my rocker boyfriend's passion and compassion, and then mesh them with my last boyfriend's sensitivity and depth . . . well, that would be one fabulous guy. Dream on, huh?

You know all those books they write about guys and girls being from separate planets? There's a reason. We women try to figure out what makes a man tick—and what makes a relationship stick. Boys are so confusing! Sometimes you want to slap them and say, "Can't you just tell me how you feel?" However, they think of us in the same light.

It is also so much more empowering to be alone than to stay in a dysfunctional relationship purely because it's comfortable.

My sister Ashley just got married to an amazing guy, Evan Bogart. When I asked her how she knew he was the one, she said, "He was everything I never knew I was really looking for in a man. Of course he had the qualities that every woman fantasizes about, but he was also kind, honest, funny, a good communicator, cute, ambitious, creative, and devoted."

My previous boyfriends all turned into "something more" at times when I wasn't looking for love—Jay in particular. I had just moved to NYC, and by *just* I mean I met him literally during my first weekend here when I interviewed at DVF. He was performing at a local bar, and it just happened. We were filming that night, so the cameras were able to catch it all (lucky us!). I took the bull by the horns and offered to buy Jay a drink after his set. We were instantly enthralled in conversation and spent the whole night dancing until I had to leave for the airport at 6:00 A.M. The time just flew by.

I had heard that New York was the place to date around 'cause men abound! But soon, I found myself in the midst of an intense relationship, on and off camera! In the few years before, while filming *The Hills,* I never let my old boyfriend be filmed. I just wanted to keep part of my life private, and now I know why it was so important. A real romance cannot survive being documented on a reality TV series. You never quite let your guard down, and you're never 100 percent honest about how you're feeling, because you're always thinking, *I can't say that because everyone is watching.*

Love is between two people; it's meant to be private.

I will never (let me say it again!) NEVER allow a serious boyfriend to be part of the show. I've learned it's a recipe for disaster. Love is between two people; it's meant to be private. You don't always know guys' motives, and to have all these opinions of strangers as well as a crew weighing in becomes too much of a burden. It totally takes the spontaneity out of a relationship. I will certainly go on dates, but if any guy I meet turns out to be someone I really want to give my heart to . . . I'm keeping him as far from the cameras as possible!

My final love lesson is communication. It's key. I feel like it's been the biggest hurdle I have had to overcome in all of my relationships, and I think a lot of girls feel this way. I always assume the man I'm dating knows precisely what I'm thinking, what I want, what is right and what is wrong, but he doesn't! *Hmmm* . . . you mean men aren't mind readers? Ladies, we have to *tell* them. We have to open up and be honest and say what we think is great and working in the relationship, and what is out of whack or just plain pissing us off. It cracks me up, because I (and most girls in general) can gab for hours with my girlfriends, analyzing every nuance of our relationships. But when it comes to a guy I'm actually involved with? I zip my lip and hope he has psychic abilities. One of the things I really need to work on is allowing myself to open up and be vulnerable.

When you want to give your guy something sweet, try one of the incredible flavors from Baked by Melissa.

WHITTYISM: GUY-WOWING GIFTS

Relationships are stressful enough . . . then comes Hanukkah, Christmas, Valentine's Day, his birthday. You can't just get your guy *any* gift. It has to show how much you know about him; it has to say "I'm the coolest, best girlfriend in the world and you are *so* lucky to have me." I have found that these gifts are definitely man-pleasers and will earn you brownie points for creativity! An added plus—they won't break your bank account.

- A DIY cupcake. Bake him a pair (one for you/one for him), then provide a "palette" of his fave toppings: chocolate frosting, whipped cream, M&Ms, Reeses, gummy worms . . . you name it. Tell him you chose this present because he's "so sweet."
- What hardworking man wouldn't love a massage . . . by you? Make it as spalike an experience as possible: dim the lights, put on soothing music, sprinkle rose petals around the room, and rub him with scented oil.
- Break out the video camera (you can ask a good friend to help if you don't have a tripod) and record him a sexy music video. Can't carry a tune? He won't notice, especially if you belt out "I'm Too Sexy" or do your best Britney impression of "Baby One More Time." He'll beg for an encore for sure!
- Play some naughty versions of childhood games. A friend of mine bought her boyfriend Twister . . . then told him they had to play it in the buff! If you're not quite as bold, there's always spin the bottle!
- Beer-of-the-month club membership. He'll think of you with every brew!
- A sweet, heartfelt note. Simple yes, but you'll wow him with your honesty and admiration. What guy wouldn't love a love letter?
- A scent. Kind of a selfish gift, but men always appreciate cologne.

MEET THE PARENTS

For some people, introducing their new boyfriend/girlfriend to their folks is no big deal. But I need a little preparation. Like the time I was on just date number two with Freddie Facklemayer. (I had met Freddie through his brother, Harry, who had invited Freddie out with us.) Freddie seemed like a nice New York boy and he was also a friend of my friend Sami. But then he surprised me by asking his dad along to dinner—when we barely knew each other. He felt totally comfortable with the introduction in the early stages of our relationship; I, on the other hand, broke out in a cold sweat. I just wasn't ready to meet his dad!

Most people feel that "meeting the parents" is a big step. It says that you're serious; you want your family to like and accept him, and you want his parents to think you're the greatest thing since Spanx. Although it's hard to know when it's the right time (that really depends on how you feel), generally three months is a good amount of time to wait before making introductions. When the time arrives—and you're face-to-face with his folks . . .

- Make sure you're dressed conservatively (not too sexy). Avoid skintight clothing, plunging necklines—basically anything sloppy or slutty. They'll be looking you over from head to toe, so make sure you're polished and put together.

- Even if your knees are knocking, be friendly and warm and try to at least look at ease. Be yourself; don't put on airs or act like someone you think they want you to be. Your integrity will impress them.

- Ask polite questions. People love to talk about themselves. Like, "I love this painting in the family room. Where did you find it?" An added plus: you'll learn lots about your boyfriend's past (maybe even details about his former girlfriends!).

- If you're going to his family's home for a meal or for an overnight, bring a token gift. Anything! A bottle of wine, a bunch of flowers, a small dessert. One summer, I went to visit my boyfriend's home in Martha's Vineyard. I knew I would be the guest of his family, and I couldn't come empty-handed. I brought some bubble-wrapped bud vases in my suitcase. When I left, I placed them in their kitchen while everyone was sleeping (I had to leave and make an early flight home). It was *very* appreciated! I also recently bought a guy friend's mom an awesome new Italian cookbook. You can never have enough cookbooks!

THE L WORD

This was a huge debate between me, Erin Lucas, and Jay: When is the right time to say "I love you" in a relationship? Erin's guy, Duncan, blurted it out before she did—and after a mere two weeks. Jay said he thinks people say it too quickly. His theory is you wait and see if it's *really* love (as opposed to infatuation). My take is if it feels right, it *is* right—no matter what the timing is for anyone else. Some guys might get scared. But what if he feels the same way? What if he's holding back on saying it to you because he fears your reaction? I say go for it, girl! There are so many great ways to say it! You don't have to make a big production out of it; just look into his eyes . . . and say it. Of course, there are cuter and more eloquent ways—like spelling out "I Love You" in jelly beans on the bed or writing it in lipstick on his bathroom mirror. Some people get all poetic—but usually that's just in the movies.

Here is one of my favorite "I love you" lines from a flick (in case you need a little inspiration):

I love that you get cold when it's seventy-one degrees out. I love that it takes you an hour and a half to order a sandwich. I love that you get a little crinkle above your nose when you're looking at me like I'm nuts. I love that after I spend the day with you, I can still smell your perfume on my clothes. And I love that you are the last person I want to talk to before I go to sleep at night.

—Billy Crystal in *When Harry Met Sally*

A GUY'S PERSPECTIVE: WHITNEY'S BEST BOY BUD, BEN

Ben and I have known each other for over a decade. We went to school together from seventh grade through sophomore year of college at the University of Colorado-Boulder, when I transferred to USC. We are constantly analyzing the opposite sex with each other; he thinks girls are crazy and I think guys are crazier! Sometimes he'll call and leave me a message, "Whit, I need your advice in the love department . . ." I do enjoy hearing his trials and tribulations, and I often ask him for insights into the male mind.

Ben's such a great friend. We are constantly gushing about our romantic endeavors/issues to each other.

4 *He gets green with envy.*

This happens every time you mention, text, or even look at another guy. I remember how freaked out Jay got when I told him I had lunch with my workmate Chris (smooth move on my part!). If even purely platonic relationships make him jealous, it indicates he wants you all to himself.

5 *He's fast-forwarding to the future.*

All of a sudden, he's quizzing you about how you see your future: Do you want to be married in a church or by Elvis in Vegas? House in the burbs or apartment in the city? How many kids? These aren't just hypotheticals or small talk; he's thinking long term and making sure you're on the same page. He's also trying to gauge your reaction—or what you're doing on a certain date within the next couple months.

6 *He wants to be with you.*

Every chance he gets! And he sacrifices his own time to be with you.

WOULD I LIE TO YOU, BABE?

Honesty is *everything* in a relationship. If there's no trust, you'll crumble as a couple. Of course, I had to find this out for myself the hard way: like when both Alex, a guy I once dated, and my friend Jess both warned me that Jay wasn't being honest about his ex, Danielle. Jay was staying with me, but coming home at five or six in the morning, and I didn't know where he was. Shouldn't I have seen the writing on the wall? Shouldn't I have figured out he was hooking up with his ex again? Part of me didn't want to admit this to myself; sometimes, it's just easier to put blinders on and not acknowledge the problems.

So how do you know if your guy lies? A lot of it is trusting your own instincts. Kelly Cutrone always says, "The truth doesn't always come like a shiny little bluebird on someone's shoulder." Sometimes you just have this feeling in the pit of your stomach. Oprah has her *aha!* moments. Well, I have my *uh-oh!* moments. These are the times a little bell goes off in the back of my brain and it tells me, "Whitney . . . wise up. Something is not right here." Unfortunately, I don't always listen. So now—sadder but wiser—here's my advice for you. Listen to your own inner voice. Don't be paranoid or accusative until you have evidence, but *do* be smart. Sometimes guys are really good at covering up what they've been up to. Jay certainly was slick in that department. But I had begun to feel a tension between us; the passion was kind of waning. And when we'd talk over dinner or drinks, and I'd tell him what a bad day at work I had, he didn't seem to care. He didn't really even seem interested. I could see his eyes avoiding mine. Telltale sign right there: if he can't look you in the eye, he's definitely hiding something from you.

When you do finally clear the air and get things out in the open, it probably won't be pretty. Jay got superdefensive when I asked him why he couldn't be honest with me. But you can't keep quiet forever because you're afraid of rocking the boat. If someone is lying to you, he doesn't respect you or care about you in a way that you deserve.

THE EX FILES

So over—that's what I thought it was with Jay. He was off on tour, out of my life, and I was just trying to move on. Then he shows up outside the DVF store during an event to tell me he's sorry and he felt bad with how we ended things. Then came the inevitable: "Whit, I made a mistake . . ." Translation: let's get back together. Forgive and forget and take me back, why don't ya? It was tempting; I had obviously been missing him, and he caught me off guard. Plus, he looked *really* hot in that black suit with that scruffy beard. He even had tears in his eyes when he said, "I love you. Better late than never . . ." I stood my ground; I told him it was too little, too late. And I meant it. I'm not the kind of girl who crumbles. When I make a decision, I stick to it—even if I wasn't 100 percent sure that he cheated.

Jay's so cute (and also has the sweetest soul). He really got me through my first year in NYC.

I know it's *so* easy to go back to someone you were once with. You have to weigh the pros and the cons: What was good about the relationship? What was bad? What needs to change and what will *never* change? What do you want in your life—and is he really a part of that picture?

Before you indulge in a blast from your past, consider this:

The reason you split.
Why did you break up in the first place? What were the issues you had, and have they been resolved? Has he really changed—or can you live with things you couldn't live with before? Make a list; check it twice.

Your head as well as your heart.
If you're swept up in emotion ("He's back! He's back!"), it's hard to see clearly. Before you agree to rekindle your relationship, give yourself time to think things through.

Your expectations for the future.
Do you think getting back together is a long-term commitment? Or are you just looking for a fun flashback?

WHITNEY 101: SIX SIGNS IT'S OVER

If your relationship is experiencing several of these, honey, you're history . . .

1 *Absence is making the heart grow colder.*

You should be able to be apart for a night or even a few days and not worry his eye (and God knows what else) is wandering. Like the time my friend Allie went on a modeling assignment and her longtime live-in boyfriend, Adam, kissed another girl. Freedom should not equal a free pass to fool around behind your back.

2 *The fire has fizzled.*

You can't remember the last time the two of you kissed, cuddled, fooled around, did *anything* besides argue.

3 *You have nothing to say.*

Literally. You stare across the table from each other at dinner, and the conversation is tense and strained. It probably should have clued me in when all Jay and I had to talk about was work, weather, and how wonderful he was.

4 *He doesn't want to make future plans.*

Major red flag: you ask him to come to a work party and he mumbles something about "a previous commitment." Then you ask about another night and he's busy as well. A boyfriend is *never* too busy to spend time with you.

5 *You don't think happy thoughts.*

When your relationship began, every time you pictured his face it made you feel all warm and fuzzy. Now when you close your eyes and see him, you see only red. And the thought of you two breaking up enters your mind every day.

6 *You're constantly fighting.*

Nothing he does is ever good enough.

Definitely not thinking very happy thoughts!

I'd love to tell you I am a person who doesn't care about how she looks—that what matters to me are only my ideas and hard work, not how my skin or hair is behaving. But that would be lying. Case in point: I woke up one morning running late to a meeting, and I had no time to shower. So I tossed my unwashed, matted hair into a messy pile on the top of my head and secured it with a butterfly clip. I tried to tell myself I looked okay—it's "casual chic"! But as I was racing out the door, I felt sloppy and greasy. I didn't even want to take another look in the mirror. I made my meeting on time, but while I was sitting in that conference room, trying to appear oh-so-serious and businesslike, I was really sending out telepathic pleas to everyone present: "Don't look at my hair! Don't look at my hair!"

There are a few freaky types who have naturally gorgeous locks and glowing skin and don't need to do much except slap on some lip gloss to look presentable. But the rest of us "mortals" need to primp and prep so we don't scare away our coworkers. I don't sanction obsessing over hair, skin care, and makeup, but I think it's worth it to spend some time and money on your upkeep so you feel good—not to mention, it's fun. In the work world, people *do* judge you on appearances. Sloppy hair and no makeup convey: "I don't care about anything . . . my work included." I think you should do whatever it takes to make yourself feel confident, beautiful, and bold. And if that means a full head of highlights or a weekly mani . . . so be it!

MY HAIR-STORY

My hair and I have had a love-hate relationship. One of the most stressful tress moments happened when I was about fifteen. I decided I wanted to go blonder, so I used one of those at-home coloring kits and left it on just a *little* too long. When I came out of the bathroom, my sister Paige gasped in horror: my hair was orange. Not a lovely Lindsay Lohan auburn red . . . that would have been tolerable. I'm talking Sunny Delight orange. Hideous. I couldn't even get an appointment at the salon to fix it for several days, so I wore a hat to school, hoping no one would notice.

Over the years, my hair has been dozens of different shades, shapes, and lengths—all in my endless quest to land on a style that I love. I was born with kind of the same hair I have now—fairly straight strawberry blond with a little curl on the bottom. When I was in high school, it was "the

blonder, the better." I wanted to look like a real beach blonde. In 2006, I cut it off to my chin—the second-hugest hair mistake in my life.

In college my hair was mostly long and blond—except for a few months where I decided chocolate brown would look good on me (it didn't; it turned green). When I look back on early episodes of *The Hills,* my hair in my sophomore year was one solid mass of platinum blond. Thankfully, I'm over that phase; it took me nearly two years to get back to my natural shade, and I am so grateful to my colorist Johnny Ramirez at Chris McMillan Salon in L.A. for painstakingly working in natural highlights and lowlights and bringing my hair back to a state of healthy shininess again. It's important to find a stylist you love and trust—he should be your "Mr. Right" of Hair. He/she should hear you and not try to force his/her "vision" on you. For years, I felt like the stylists I was using just didn't get what I was saying: "Guys, I want my hair to look real!" Finally, Johnny listened—and he assured me he'd grant my hair wish, if I was patient and let him do it in baby steps (you can't erase years of bleaching trauma overnight).

These days, my hair is pretty long, thick, and wavy. I love the length and want to grow it even longer—but it's not low maintenance. Long hair knots easily and can get fried from coloring, styling, and sitting in the sun. Through much trial and error—and my hair paying the price—I have finally settled on a hair-care regimen that I like and that works for me. I love Enjoy Luxury shampoo and conditioner. It comes in hot pink bottles (very me!), and my cousin Jackie Braverman is a stylist in Vegas and sends me big tubs of it. I get my hair done so frequently for the show, dates, and appearances, the hot tools annihilate my hair. These products make it feel so soft and healthy again. I

also use Frédéric Fekkai protein cream. I brush it through my hair and douse it on the tips at night before I fall asleep. It just sinks in, and when I wake up in the morning, my hair feels reborn! I also just got this Mason Pearson boar paddle brush, which was really pricey, but a good investment. The natural bristles polish the hair, laying the cuticle flat to make the hair shine—and it doesn't tear my hair out like some hard vinyl bristle brushes do. And I just found a great new product: Moroccan oil. It's a great leave-in conditioner that smells good, and a little goes a long way.

The important thing is to find products that work for your hair—not for your roomie, your mother, or that A-lister who flaunts her fabulous mane in ads. It's very personal—as personal as picking your own wardrobe. There are some general guidelines you can follow, based on hair type (see the next section), but in the end, you should settle on what makes your hair feel healthy, shiny, bouncy, and so on. I say experiment! If someone gives me a new product or I see a small sample bottle at the drugstore, I'll give it a whirl. It may not do wonders for my hair . . . but then again, it could be the magic potion I've been searching for.

This is me with just moisturizer and some tinted face cream.

My Five-Minute Face

I'm a big fan of a simple look, and since we don't have a makeup artist on *The City*, I've learned to do my own . . . fast! I know this seems like a lot of steps, but I can do it in just five minutes flat.

Step 1: I start by mixing Fresh High Noon tinted moisturizer with the Fresh Soy Face Cream to get a nice base with a sun-kissed glow.

Step 2: Next I brush on Bare Minerals powder with SPF 15 to even out my skin.

I cringe just th
wasn't bad enou
send me chocol
to get me throug

For dinner, I
the street to Cl
times a week and

Step 3: Then I bronze with Guerlain Number One for Blondes on my cheeks, hairline, and jawline.

Step 4: I sweep a little Nars Orgasm blush on my cheekbones, forehead, nose, and chin.

Step 5: I use Anastasia Brow Gel to give my eyebrows a nice shape (this is especially helpful if I haven't had time to go in to get them done). I highlight under my eyebrows with Benefit Eye Bright and then curl my lashes with a Sephora eyelash curler. Sometimes if I'm really feeling like going all out for the day, I put on DiorShow mascara.

Step 6: Slick on some Fresh Sugar Lip Balm and I'm good to go!

Showing on the Runway

No one will know how great your collection is unless you show it. So twice a year, we try to organize a presentation or runway show to unveil my latest designs. I recently took part in the Gen Art Fresh Faces in Fashion show in Miami where I showed my Fall 2010 collection—along with five other new designers—to a huge crowd. Although the idea of putting on a runway show sounds glam, a lot of hard work and detail go into it. At a show, the designer does much more than create the clothing; she or he has to see the entire show through production. I have to cast the models; decide on hair, makeup, lighting, and music; style all the looks with accessories; arrange for the line to be transported; send out invites; and make the all-important call—who gets to sit in the front two rows of the show. *Phew!* To get everything perfect, we do a run-through. And even then, when the real show rolls around, it's chaos backstage! My heart is always racing, but I try to focus on things going smoothly—not my nerves. Besides, I really don't have time to worry—the show flies by in about fifteen to twenty minutes.

Backstage and onstage at the Gen Art show.

Hitting the Stores

Immediately after the show, my samples get sent to the showroom that carries my line for buyers to look at or the sales team takes them on the road for me, bringing them to boutiques, department stores, and trade conventions (Project is the big one in Vegas; Coterie in New York City). Hopefully, they get lots of orders and that helps us determine how much to produce. When I actually see my looks on racks or shelves in stores . . . that's the ultimate reward!

Promotion/Branding

Even though you may have a great line, you can't assume people will just know about it and wear it. Press and promotion is a huge part of being a successful designer and you have to cover all your bases. This year, I redesigned my entire Web site (whitneyeve.com) top to bottom. I wanted it to reflect more of the vibe of my clothing. Before, the site was a bit too flowery and old-fashioned. Now I think it's feminine-chic and very modern—I love it!

But the Internet isn't the only way to get the word out. At my PR offices, we do a press preview day. We set up a time for all the editors from the monthlies and weeklies to come and look at my new collection. The goal is simple: I want them to incorporate my line into their fashion editorial. Being able to say you were in *Elle, Seventeen,* or *Glamour* really gives you credibility as a designer. An editor from *Glamour* came by and chose one of my skirts to be featured on their "Nice Price" page. They styled an entire look around my watercolor chiffon mini from my Spring 2010 collection. And Joe Zee, the creative director of *Elle,* was pulling together a "Black, White, and Red" feature and asked me to send over my entire Fall 2010 collection. *Twilight* star Ashley Greene is going to be the model for the story, so my fingers are crossed that a lot of it will make it into the mag. Ya never know . . .

I was so proud and happy when the show was over. I still have to pinch myself sometimes: I'm really a designer!